THE SECRET

Discovering God's Secret Of Handling Money

MOODY PUBLISHERS

CHICAGO

CONTENTS

3 5 7 9 10 8 6 4 2

© Copyright 1997 by Crown Ministries, Inc.

Unless otherwise noted, Scripture quotation are from the *New American Standard Bible,* copyright 1960, 1962, 1963, 1968, 1971, 1973, 1975, 1975, 1977 by the Lockman Foundation.

Verses identified as NIV are taken from the *Holy Bible: New International Version,* copyright 1973, 1978, 1984, by the International Bible Society. Used by permission of Zondervan Bible Publishers.

Verses identified as LB as taken from *The Living Bible,* 1971 by Tyndale House Publishers. Used by permission.

ISBN 0-8024-3154-2 - Printed in Italy

Welcome

**You are about to start the exciting journey
of discovering God's secret of handling money.**

At the end of each chapter you will do some fun things that will help you now and for the rest of your life. Here they are—

Memorize this verse!

The best way to remember God's truth is to memorize it. So you will memorize one special verse at the end of each chapter.

Answer these questions!

You will think about and write down your answers to some great questions.

Work it out!

Next you will do something that will really help you with your money — like opening a savings account.

Pray for me!

Now, this will be exciting! You will write down what other people want you to pray about for them. And they will write down your prayer requests. Then you will pray for each other every day — and watch God answer your prayers!

Grandpa and Abigail

Now, remember," the coach said, "you have six weeks to get enough money for baseball camp. This camp will be the best seven days of your life!"

"Oh, sure," Josh whispered to Andy. "If we can come up with the money!"

Andy groaned, "How will we ever be able to do it?"

Coach Stevens was reminding everyone to pick up their bats and gloves as Maria and Ruth came running over.

"Can you believe that?" Maria said excitedly. "Three major league players are going to be at camp. Just think how much we will learn about baseball."

Ruth picked up Josh's glove and tossed it to him. "Didn't you tell us your grandpa used to play baseball with the Red Sox, Josh?" she asked.

Josh flung his bag over his shoulder as the four friends walked to their bikes. "Yes, he played with them for five years and was an all-star," Josh answered. With a frown he continued, "But I'm not sure I'll be able to go. Camp costs a lot and I don't know where I'm going to get the money."

"Me, either," Andy said. "My dad's been out of work for two months, and Mom said it's hard right now just to put food on the table."

"I'm not sure I'll have it either," added Ruth. Suddenly she grabbed Maria's arm. "I've got an idea," she said. "Why don't we find a way to earn enough money to pay for camp?"

"How are we going to do that?" Maria asked dejectedly. "What can four eleven-year-old kids do to earn all that money?"

"I know what we can do," Josh interrupted. "Let's go over to my grandpa's house. I want you to meet him. Maybe he will have some good

ideas. He's real smart!"

"Let's go," the others said. They jumped on their bikes and took off down the street.

Josh's grandparents had just moved to town. Josh's grandpa was a veterinarian who had taken care of farm animals. They had moved so they could be closer to Josh and his family.

"This is it!" Josh called out as he turned his bike into the driveway of an old white farmhouse on the edge of town. The fence around the large field behind the barn was old and broken down.

Andy, Ruth and Maria followed, coming to a stop under a big maple tree in the front yard. They jumped off their bikes and spotted Josh's grandpa coming out of the barn. Three chickens scrambled out of the barn behind him, chased by a calico cat.

Grandpa stood there in faded blue jeans and a red plaid flannel shirt. White hair stuck out from under his Red Sox baseball cap. As he smiled, his eyes twinkled.

"Hi, Grandpa," Josh called as he ran up and gave him a hug. Grandpa's big hands wrapped around Josh as he swung him in a circle.

As Grandpa put him down, Josh tumbled to the ground. Just then a large black and tan German shepherd ran up with his tail wagging. He licked Josh's face. Everyone laughed as Josh wiped his cheeks.

"Samson couldn't wait to see you face-to-face again, Josh," Grandpa said with a laugh.

Josh sat up and hugged Samson. "You're a good dog," he said. "My friends will like you a lot."

"Well, you've all met Samson," Grandpa said. "You can call me Grandpa Pete. But I don't know your names yet. How about introducing me to your friends, Josh?"

"This is Andy, Maria and Ruth," Josh said. Just then the calico cat rubbed up against Andy's legs. Surprised, he jumped away.

Grandpa laughed. "That's Patches coming over to meet you," he said. Ruth and Maria knelt down and started petting Patches.

Just then Josh's grandma stepped out onto the back porch. "Hi, Josh," she called. "I'm glad you brought your friends over. I'm making lemonade. I'll bring you some in a minute."

"Thanks, Grandma," Josh answered. Then he turned to Grandpa, asking, "Where's Abigail, Grandpa?"

"She's in the field out back," Grandpa answered. "Come on, kids, I'll introduce you to Abigail."

Josh ran over to the gate with the others close behind. Josh pointed to a little hut with straw on the ground. "That's where she is," he called back to his friends.

"Look at this," Maria exclaimed as she arrived. There, on her side, lay a huge pig, her pink belly sticking out like a watermelon. She lifted her head and grunted when she saw the kids, but didn't make another move.

Maria stooped down next to Abigail and started to pet the pig's head, but she then stopped and looked at Grandpa. "Will she bite me?" she asked.

"Probably not, but be careful," Grandpa cautioned. "Abigail's going to have some baby pigs in about three weeks. She's gotten so big she's uncomfortable and a little grouchy. Try scratching behind her ears. She loves that."

Andy moved closer to Grandpa. "There's no way I'm going to touch that fat old pig!" he said, pushing his hands deep into his pockets.

"Well," Grandpa said, putting his arm around Andy's shoulders. "It's wise to be careful until you get to know strange animals."

"Grandpa, when are you going to bring your horses from Ohio?" Josh asked.

"Just as soon as I can repair the broken-down fence," replied Grandpa. "Horses need a fence to keep them where they belong, you know."

"I don't know any more about farm animals than I do about getting enough money for baseball camp," Josh groaned. "Grandpa, that's one of the reasons we came to see you. Our coach told us about camp this morning. It's going to be so much fun! There's even going to be three major league players there. But we only have six weeks to get enough money to go. Our parents won't be able to help us very much. Can you think of some ways we could earn some money?"

Andy looked up at Grandpa and said, "We'd do anything to go to camp. We just don't know what to do!"

"Well, I know a good place for you to start finding out about money," Grandpa said.

"Where?" they asked in unison.

"Right here," Grandpa said, pulling out a thin, black book from his shirt pocket. "I carry this with me all the time because it has the answers to a lot of my problems."

"Grandpa, that's the Bible," Josh exclaimed. "What can it tell us about earning money to go to camp?"

Grandpa smiled as he pulled off his baseball cap. "I've spent years studying what God says about money, and believe me, He says a lot. Did you know there are more than 2,350 verses in the Bible that talk about money?"

Josh was growing impatient. "But, Grandpa, we need to know how to earn money," he said, a frown wrinkling up the freckles on his nose. "If we don't, we'll never make it to camp."

"I understand, Josh," Grandpa answered. "I'll make a deal with you kids. If you let me teach you some of the things that God says about the way we should handle money, then I will help you figure out some ways to earn enough money for camp. There will be twelve lessons. Before each lesson you'll need to look up some Bible verses and answer some questions. You'll also memorize a Bible verse for each lesson. And if you will help me fix this broken-down fence and take care of Abigail and the other animals, I'll pay you for your work."

"Will you really?" Maria said. "It would be so exciting if we could go to camp."

"Is it a deal, then?" Grandpa asked, standing up and brushing the straw from his jeans.

"Sure, it's a deal!" said Josh, sounding excited for the first time since the coach told them about the baseball camp.

Just then they heard the back door open. Grandma came out carrying a tray. "Who's ready for some lemonade?" she asked.

"I am!" all four kids shouted as Grandma set the tray down on a bale of hay.

"Grandpa," Josh asked, "can we start right now on our first lesson?"

"Well, this is as good a time as any," said Grandpa. He paused and looked over at Maria and Ruth sitting on the straw beside Abigail. "Look at Abigail. As soon as Maria and Ruth started scratching her ears she started smiling at them."

Abigail was so contented with the girls' attention that she had fallen asleep. With her closed eyes and turned-up snout she looked like she was smiling. The boys laughed, and Andy ventured over to sit beside her. Gingerly he reached over to scratch her ear, then pulled his hand away as she grunted loudly.

Grandpa laughed and continued, "There are three things I'd like you to remember from this lesson. The first is that God says a lot about how we should handle money. Remember, there are 2,350 verses in the Bible that talk about money. Why do you think the Lord said so much about money? He wanted to give us clear directions for how to use it. He wanted to help us avoid making mistakes in handling it.

"The second thing I'd like you to remember is that God's way for us to handle money is different from the way most people handle money. God tells us in Isaiah 55:8-9: *My thoughts are not your thoughts, neither are your ways My ways.* The Bible tells us all about God's ways, and that includes how we should handle money."

"We'll be able to remember that, Grandpa," said Josh. "What's the last thing we should know?"

Grandpa took out his Bible and turned to Luke 16:11. "Andy, why don't you read Luke 16:11 for us?"

"Sure," said Andy. *"If therefore you have not been faithful in the use of worldly wealth, who will entrust the true riches to you?"*

"That's a little harder to understand, kids," said Grandpa. "But this is what it means. If you handle your money the way the Lord wants you to, you will become closer friends with God. The joys and blessings of knowing Him well are the 'true riches' mentioned in that verse.

"After practice tomorrow, come over and we'll look at the second lesson," Grandpa said. "We'll study what part God plays with our money. In a minute I'll make a list of the verses for you to look up and the questions for you to answer. I'll also tell you which verse to memorize. Why, in six weeks you'll be getting on the bus to go to camp." Then he asked with a twinkle in his eyes, "Say, Josh, do you think they need an old Red Sox player to attend your camp?"

Memorize this scripture!

If therefore you have not been faithful in the use of worldly wealth, who will entrust the true riches to you? (Luke 16:11).

Answer these questions!

1. Open the Bible and read *Isaiah 55:8-9.* Do you think God's way of handling money is different from the way most people handle money? _____

_____

_____

_____

2. What do you think would be the greatest difference?

_____

_____

_____

_____

3. There are more than 2,350 verses in the Bible that talk about money. Why do you think the Lord says so much about money?

_____

_____

_____

4. Look up and read *Luke 16:11*. What do you think are the "true riches" the Lord mentions in this verse? _____

_____

_____

_____

Work it out! If you do not have a Bible, get one so you can look up what God says about money. Read over the books of the Bible listed in the front of your Bible — they start with Genesis and end with Revelation. Some of the books are in the Old Testament and some are in the New Testament.

Count the books in the Bible. How many are there? _____

Get ready for the next chapter! Memorize *1 Chronicles 29:11-12* and answer the questions on pages 19 and 20.

Pray for me! Share your prayer requests with one another and write them down on the Prayer Lists beginning on page 104. Then end the lesson by praying.

CHAPTER 2

A Giant in the Clubhouse

"Come on, Maria, I'll beat you to Grandpa's," Josh called as he pedaled his bike down the road. Andy and Ruth were close behind. They had just finished baseball practice and were heading over to Grandpa's house.

Earlier that morning Grandpa had called Josh and said, "Morning, Josh. I wanted to catch you before you left home. I've got a surprise for you and your friends!"

No matter how hard he tried, that's all Josh could get Grandpa to tell him. He had no idea what the surprise was, but he was anxious to find out. The kids turned into the driveway and coasted to the back yard. They jumped off their bikes just as Grandpa walked out of the barn carrying some fence posts.

"About time you got here," he called. Samson ran up to the kids, wagging his tail.

"Grandpa, tell us about the surprise," Josh begged impatiently.

"Whoa, Josh, you're always in a hurry. You remind me of a feisty, young colt I used to have," Grandpa replied. "Come on over to the barn. The surprise is in there."

The kids ran for the barn. They stopped at the doorway as Josh exclaimed, "Look what Grandpa built for us!"

Grandpa had set up a clubhouse in one corner of the barn. A piece of tan canvas was attached to the center beam of the roof and stretched across to the wall. Under the canvas Grandpa had put five or six bales of hay and a couple of old upside-down crates. The hay smelled like fresh cut grass. A sign painted with the words "Clubhouse" was nailed to the wall. A rope hung from the roof of the barn with knots tied about every eighteen inches apart.

The kids ran over to the hay, sending a big brown hen scurrying off one of the bales. The hen squawked loudly. "I guess that hen wanted to use that hay for her roost," Grandpa said laughing.

Josh grabbed a knot on the rope and swung in circles. "This is great, Grandpa," he said.

"Why don't you climb on up to the loft, Josh?" Grandpa asked,

14

pointing to the loft near the roof where the rope had been tied.

Josh, then Andy, climbed up the knots and stepped onto the loft. Some of the boards creaked. Then they sat down on the edge, sticking their legs under the railing.

"This is a great place for a clubhouse, Grandpa Pete," said Maria. "We can come here every day after we help with the animals. Thanks so much for making it for us."

"You're welcome," Grandpa said. "I thought this would be a good place for me to teach you what God says about money."

"It's great," said Josh. "But we can't tell anybody else about it, gang. It's our clubhouse. It belongs just to us!"

"Not really," said Ruth. "It belongs to Grandpa Pete. He's just letting us use it."

"Well, you're not quite right about that, Ruth," Grandpa said, "I don't really own the barn or the house or the animals."

"You don't?" Andy questioned. "Then who does?"

"Why don't you and Josh come on down and I'll tell you all about it," Grandpa answered.

After the boys climbed down the rope, Grandpa said, "Now let me tell you about the owner of the clubhouse."

Grandpa reached in his pocket and pulled out the little Bible. He opened it up and said, "In this lesson I want you to learn what part God plays with our money. There are three things that are important to understand. The first is that the Lord owns everything. Listen to this, *The earth is the Lord's, and everything in it, the world, and all who live in it* (Psalm 24:1, NIV).

"God owns this clubhouse," Grandpa said. "He owns my house, my animals, your houses, your bikes — why, God even owns us. God owns everything. The Bible even lists some of the things that the Lord owns. In Leviticus 25:23 the Bible tells us He owns the land, and Haggai 2:8 tells us He owns the silver and gold. Psalm 50:10-11 says, *Every animal of the forest is already mine, the cattle on a thousand hills are mine . . . every living thing in the fields is mine.*"

They sat quietly thinking about Grandpa's words. Andy broke the silence. "I guess that means the Lord owns Abigail the pig?"

"Yes, Andy, and pretty soon the Lord is going to own some baby pigs," Grandpa said with a smile.

Andy whistled softly and shook his head. "Now I see what you meant when you told us that God's ways are different than ours. We never would have known He was the owner of everything if the Bible hadn't told us."

Grandpa nodded his head. "Now the second part is really special. God is in control of everything that happens to you. Knowing the Lord is in control helps us to be at peace when things seem to go wrong. It gives us courage when we are faced with problems."

"Like our getting enough money to go to camp," said Ruth.

Grandpa smiled, "What you kids are facing reminds me of a story in the Bible about a boy just about your age who dealt with a giant problem."

"You're talking about David, aren't you?" Maria interrupted.

"Yes, Maria," Grandpa answered. "David was just a young boy taking care of his fathers' sheep. Did you know that he killed both a lion and a bear when they tried to attack the sheep? How would you like to face a hungry bear all by yourself?"

"But he wasn't all by himself," Andy said. "God was with him!"

"You're right, Andy," Grandpa exclaimed.

"Tell us about the giant," Ruth said.

"Sure," Grandpa answered. "The whole army of Israel was afraid of a giant named Goliath who was over nine feet tall!" Suddenly, Grandpa jumped to his feet and said, "Follow me."

Over in a corner Grandpa had stacked bales of hay nine feet high in the shape of a person. "Stand next to the hay so you can see how big Goliath was," he told the kids.

"Wow!" Andy said with a whistle.

"David's older brothers were soldiers in the army, and David's father sent him to take some food to his brothers. When David arrived, he found that everyone was terrified of Goliath.

"Every day for forty days Goliath shouted to the Israelites, 'Choose a man and let us fight each other. If he kills me, we will become your slaves; but if I kill him, you will be our slaves.' But they were so afraid of Goliath that no one would fight him.

"However, David was brave because he knew God was in control of even Goliath. He remembered how God had taken care of him when he faced a bear and lion. So he volunteered to fight Goliath. Imagine a young boy fighting a nine-foot giant!"

"What happened?" Andy asked, his eyes big with excitement.

"David took a smooth stone and put it in a sling," Grandpa said as he started to swing an imaginary sling over his head. Then Grandpa shouted, "Goliath, you come to fight me with a sword and a spear, but I come in the name of the Lord." Grandpa threw the imaginary stone at the straw Goliath.

"The stone struck the giant in the head and he fell over dead. Come on, kids, help me knock over Goliath!" The kids giggled as they ran over to help Grandpa push the bales to the ground.

Grandpa brushed the straw off his shirt and continued. "Now, here's the most important part of the story. Listen to what David said many years after he killed that giant. *Everything in the heavens and earth is yours, O Lord, and this is your kingdom. We adore you as being in control of everything* (1 Chronicles 29:11, LB).

"Even though David had become a great and powerful king, he still knew God was the owner of everything and in control of everything."

Grandpa stopped, lifted his baseball cap off his head and wiped his forehead on his sleeve. "Whew, I forgot how much work it was to tell a story."

Ruth laughed and said, "Especially when you *show and tell* the story!"

Then Josh said, "Grandpa, God owns everything, and He controls everything. What is the third thing God does?"

Grandpa continued, "He promises to meet our needs. Look over there by the door at those three black crows eating the chicken feed off the ground. Those crows remind me of the ravens that brought bread and meat to Elijah every morning and evening during a famine.

"Elijah was God's prophet. But he found himself in the middle of a famine. There was no food anywhere. But God used ravens to bring food to him every day. God never let him down. And He won't let you down either.

"Now, I want to make another deal with you," said Grandpa with a smile. "I want to help you discover a secret. I'm going to give you several clues during our lessons that will help you discover God's secret of handling money. If you can guess the secret before it's time to go to camp, I'll pay half of the cost of camp for each of you."

"Really!" exclaimed Maria. "You'd do that for us? What's the first clue?"

Grandpa smiled, "The first clue is this—when you discover the secret, it will mean even more to you than going to camp."

After the kids thought about Grandpa's clue, he added, "Come early tomorrow. We'll work together to start repairing the fence so that we can bring the horses. You will be able to earn more money by taking care of them."

Josh gave Grandpa a hug and said, "Thanks again for building our clubhouse." Then with a puzzled look he said to his friends, "The first clue is hard to believe. What could mean more to us than going to camp?"

Memorize this scripture!

Everything in the heavens and earth is yours, O Lord, and this is your kingdom. We adore you as being in control of everything. Riches and honor come from you alone and you are the Ruler of all mankind: your hand controls power and might, and it is at your discretion that men are made great and given strength (1 Chronicles 29:11-12, LB).

Answer these questions!

1. Read *1 Corinthians 10:26*. Who owns everything in the world?

_____

_____

2. Name some of your things that God owns.

_____

_____

3. Read *1 Chronicles 29:11-12*. Who controls everything that happens?

_____

_____

4. List the things people need to live a normal life.

_____

_____

_____

5. Read *Matthew 6:31-33* and *Philippians 4:19*. What do these verses say about God taking care of your needs? _____

_____

_____

_____

6. Give an example from the Bible of the Lord providing for someone's needs.

_____

_____

_____

_____

7. What was the most interesting thing you learned from reading this chapter?_____

_____

_____

_____

Work it out! The first step in learning to handle money is to know how much money you get and how much you spend. Write down what you receive and spend each week.

Money I RECEIVE:

Allowance   _____

Chores   _____

Jobs   _____

Gifts   _____

Other income   _____

Total I receive for week	_____

Money I SPEND:

Giving   _____

Entertainment   _____

Food   _____

Clothes   _____

Music   _____

Sports   _____

Other spending   _____

Total I spend for week	_____

Do you spend more money than you receive? _____

If so, how much more do you spend? _____

Get ready for the next chapter! Memorize *1 Corinthians 4:2* and answer the questions on pages 27 and 28.

Pray for me! Share your prayer requests with one another and write them down on the Prayer Lists. Then end the lesson by praying.

CHAPTER 3

Fixing the Fence

Bright and early Saturday morning the four friends biked over to help Grandpa repair his fence. Just as they rode into the driveway, Grandpa stepped out of the barn with something in his hands. As they ran up to him, Andy exclaimed, "What have you got?"

Grandpa smiled as he answered, "Good morning. I've been getting ready to put my four little carpenters to work on the fence. Here's a carpenter's apron for each one of you."

He handed each of them a cloth apron that tied around their waist. Grandpa had hung a hammer from a loop on each apron. The pockets of each apron were filled with nails.

"Wow, this is neat!" said Andy as he tied his apron around his waist.

"That's the new fencing we will put up this morning," said Grandpa, pointing to a pile of boards. "Let me explain what I want you to do." They listened carefully as he explained how to repair the fence. Then they went to work.

They worked steadily for two hours. The sun was high in the sky by the time they heard Grandma calling, "It's time to take a break. I've got some cold lemonade for you. Come on over to the picnic table."

"Boy, that sounds good," Josh said, wiping his forehead on his sleeve.

The kids raced ahead of Grandpa to the table. They were already drinking their lemonade by the time he got there.

"We've got a lot done," Josh exclaimed. "I've used more than half my nails."

Grandpa smiled. "Yes, all of you have worked hard this morning. You've been faithful stewards."

"Grandpa, what's a steward?" asked Maria.

"A steward is someone who takes care of another person's things," answered Grandpa. "Another name for a steward is manager. Today, you are my stewards. You are taking care of my fence by repairing it.

"But all of us are God's stewards. We already learned that He is the owner of everything. Let me read 1 Corinthians 4:2," Grandpa said pulling out his Bible. "*Moreover it is required in stewards, that a man be found faithful* (KJV). You see, the Lord wants us to be faithful stewards who take good care of His possessions.

"We'll talk more about that after lunch. But now, let's get back to work," Grandpa said, smiling.

They worked hard the rest of the morning. By the time they used up all their nails, Grandma was calling them back to the picnic table for lunch. Grandpa said, "We're now halfway finished with the fence. You have done more than I expected you to do today. You were faithful."

"Thanks, Grandpa," said Josh. "But I'm starting to think that another word for 'faithful' is 'sore.'" He rubbed his shoulder as he spoke. "I think every muscle in my arm hurts."

"Me, too," laughed Ruth.

After lunch they picked up their hammers and carpenter aprons and headed to the clubhouse. "Tell us more about being a steward, Grandpa," Josh said.

"Remember in our last lesson we learned about the part that God plays with money," he replied. "Now we're going to learn about what we are supposed to do with money. You and I are stewards. Who remembers what a steward is?"

"A manager," answered Andy.

"That's right," said Grandpa. "We are managers of God's possessions, and He wants us to be faithful to handle them in a certain way. God wants us to earn money, spend money, save money and give money His way. And where can we find out His ways?"

"In the Bible," said Ruth.

"That's right," said Grandpa, smiling. Turning the pages of his Bible Grandpa continued, "The first thing that's important to understand is Hebrews 4:13. It says, *Nothing in all creation is hidden from God's sight. Everything is uncovered and laid bare before the eyes of him to whom we must give account* (NIV). This verse means that the Lord sees everything you do and knows everything you think.

"Did you understand the last part of that verse? It says the Lord looks at everything we do. Someday the Lord will reward those who know Him for all the things they do right, like handling money His way. Let me read 2 Corinthians 5:9-10 to you," Grandpa said, thumbing through his Bible. *"So we make it our goal to please him…For we must all appear before the judgment seat of Christ, that each one may receive what is due him for the things done while in the body, whether good or bad* (NIV)."

"Grandpa, God knows everything I do and say?" Maria asked with her eyes wide.

"Yes, He does, Maria," Grandpa answered gently. "And that would be scary except that He loves us so much. He gave us the Bible as a map to show us how to handle money the right way."

"Well, handling money is easy for me," said Andy. "I don't have very much."

"Andy," said Grandpa. "The Lord wants us to be faithful, no matter what we have. It doesn't matter if we have a thousand dollars, or only one dollar. We are to be faithful with what we have. If you are faithful with a little thing, God knows He can trust you to take care of bigger things. Andy, why don't you read Luke 16:10 for us?" Grandpa asked, handing him the Bible.

"Sure," said Andy as he turned the pages. *"He who is faithful in a very little thing is faithful also in much."*

"Thank you, Andy," said Grandpa. "That is a good verse to remind us to do a good job with little things.

"There's one more thing you should know about being a steward," he continued. "You must take care of other people's things before you can expect the Lord to give you things of your own. Let me read Luke 16:12

to you, *And if you have not been faithful in the use of that which is another's, who will give you that which is your own?*

"Because you were faithful working on the fence," said Grandpa, "I will pay you money that you can save for camp. And now is a good time for you to begin learning how to budget your money."

"Grandpa, what's a budget?" asked Josh.

"A budget is a plan that helps you spend money wisely. It will help you get what is important to you," Grandpa answered.

"Like going to camp?" Ruth questioned.

"That's right, Ruth," Grandpa replied. "Because going to camp is important to you, you must be careful not to spend your money on other things that are not as important.

"I've made something that will help you begin to budget," he continued as he began picking jars out of a box. "I want each of you to have three of these jars. One is labeled Giving, another Saving and the last Spending.

"When you receive money, decide how much you want to give and put it in the jar labeled Giving. Put the amount you plan on saving in the Saving jar and what you want to spend in the Spending jar. This way you can count the money any time in your Saving jar to find out how much more you need for camp. And you will always know how much you can spend just by looking at the Spending jar."

"But what happens when the Spending jar is empty and I want to buy something?" asked Andy.

"You will need to wait until you get money to put in the Spending jar," replied Josh.

"That's right," said Grandpa, smiling. "You don't want to take it out of the Giving or Saving jars."

"This is a great idea!" exclaimed Maria. "I can see why I've never been able to save before. I've always spent all my money. I have never saved to buy the things that are really important."

"Maria, you have just taken a big step toward going to camp," said Grandpa. "Remember, using these jars to budget will help you to become a faithful steward."

Memorize this scripture!

Moreover it is required in stewards, that a man be found faithful (1 Corinthians 4:2, KJV).

Answer these questions!

1. Look up the word *steward* in the dictionary. What does it mean?

_____

_____

_____

2. Read *1 Corinthians 4:2*. According to this verse what are stewards required to do? _____

_____

_____

_____

3. Look up *Luke 16:10*. Why do you think it is important to be faithful with small things? _____

_____

_____

_____

_____

4. Read *Luke 16:1-2*. Why did the master remove the unfaithful steward from his job? _____

_____

_____

_____

5. Read *Hebrews 4:13*. Does the Lord see everything you do? How will knowing this help you change any of the ways you act and spend money?

_____

_____

_____

_____

_____

6. Read *2 Corinthians 5:9-10*. What will happen to us in the future? Why is this important for us to understand? _____

_____

_____

_____

Work it out!

Get three jars, three cans or three small boxes and label one *Giving,* one *Saving* and one *Spending*. Decide how much you want to put in each one when you receive the money.

For the next two weeks, write in the space below how much money you received and how much you put in *Giving*, *Saving* and *Spending*.

Money I receive	*Giving*	*Saving*	*Spending*
_____	_____	_____	_____
_____	_____	_____	_____
_____	_____	_____	_____
_____	_____	_____	_____
_____	_____	_____	_____
_____	_____	_____	_____
_____	_____	_____	_____
_____	_____	_____	_____
_____	_____	_____	_____
_____	_____	_____	_____
_____	_____	_____	_____
_____	_____	_____	_____
_____	_____	_____	_____
_____	_____	_____	_____
_____	_____	_____	_____
_____	_____	_____	_____

Get ready for the next chapter! Memorize *Proverbs 22:7* and answer the questions found on pages 36 and 37.

Pray for me! Share your prayer requests with one another and write them down on the Prayer Lists. Then end the lesson by praying.

CHAPTER 4

The Oil Didn't Stop

osh had just finished cleaning out Abigail's pen and was ready to fill it with fresh straw when Andy wheeled his bike into the drive.

"Where have you been?" Josh called, grabbing a pitchfork.

Andy picked up an armload of fresh straw and hurried to help Josh. "My big brother, Eddie, bought a new CD player," Andy exclaimed. "And guess what? Eddie said he will sell me his old CD player. And he even offered to sign me up with a music club so I can get a new CD every month."

Josh threw the pitchfork down. "Well, that's just great, Andy," he said disgustedly. "We're trying to save money to go to camp, and you're going to spend your money on a CD player."

"You didn't wait to hear the best part," Andy said. "Eddie said I can pay him just a little each month until I get it paid for. And I can charge the CDs I order from the record club and pay them only a small amount each month."

Ruth and Maria had been putting fresh straw in the chickens' roosts and walked over to the boys just as Andy told Josh about charging the CDs each month.

"Oooh, Andy, that might not be such a good idea," said Ruth. "My parents are always talking about how hard it is to pay what they owe. They say they wish they had never started borrowing."

Andy answered back, a touch of hurt in his voice, "Ruth, I'm just talking about a CD player and some CDs."

Maria headed for the barn. "I think we ought to ask Grandpa what he thinks," she called.

"That's a good idea," Josh called back. "It's time to meet Grandpa in

the clubhouse anyway."

Samson joined them as they sat down.

Andy laughed as Samson licked his nose. "You understand what a good chance this is for me, don't you, boy?" he said to the dog, wrapping his arms around Samson. Everyone laughed as the big dog barked softly.

The kids heard Grandpa's voice. "What's this about a good chance?" he asked as he walked into the barn.

Grandpa listened carefully as Andy told him about his brother's offer. Andy's eyes shimmered with excitement as he asked, "Isn't it great? I can still use most of the money to go to camp and I won't have to pay all the money to Eddie for my CD player until later."

When Andy finished, Grandpa pulled out the little Bible from his shirt pocket, turned a few pages, and then kindly said, "Andy, listen to this verse and then tell me what you think it means. *Just as the rich rule the poor, so the borrower is servant to the lender* (Proverbs 22:7, LB)."

Andy listened to Grandpa read with a puzzled expression on his face. "I don't know," he answered. "It says something about servants who borrow."

"I know," Ruth said. "It says if you borrow money from someone, you become that person's servant."

"That's exactly what it means," Grandpa replied. "Until you pay off a debt you owe, a part of the money you earn will have to be paid to the lender. Let's take a look at what the Bible says about debt.

"Josh, look up Romans 13:8 and read it to us."

Josh read aloud, "*Keep out of debt and owe no man anything* (Amplified). Grandpa, this says not to owe anything to anyone," he commented when he finished.

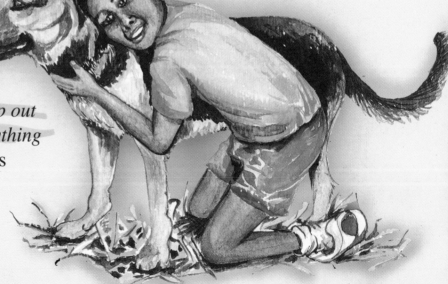

"That's right," Grandpa agreed. "That's because we become their servants just as we read a minute ago. In the Old Testament, if God's people obeyed Him, God said that one of their rewards would be that they would not be in debt."

He turned to Ruth. "That's what verses 1, 2 and 12 in Deuteronomy 28 tell us. Ruth, will you read them to us?"

Ruth read, *"If you will diligently obey the Lord . . . all these blessings shall come upon you . . . you shall lend to many nations, but you shall not borrow."*

"Later in the same chapter the Lord said that when they disobeyed, they borrowed money and got into debt," said Grandpa.

"But sometimes you have to owe people for some things, don't you? My dad's always talking about our house payment," Andy protested.

Grandpa smiled. "You're right, Andy. There might be times when it is all right to borrow money, such as when you buy a house. But there is a big difference between acting wisely by working hard to earn the money you need and acting unwisely by always charging things on credit.

"Two of the biggest reasons people borrow money is that they aren't satisfied with what they have. They want something better right away. What are some of the things that each of you would like to have right now?"

"The money to go to camp," Josh said.

"I'd like a new guitar now," said Ruth. "My music teacher said I could play a lot better if I had a new one."

"I'd like a new pair of baseball shoes," added Maria. "My old ones are black, and I'd like some white ones."

"And I'd like a brand new CD player of my own," Andy said. "Then I wouldn't have to buy Eddie's old one."

"Those are good examples," said Grandpa. "Each of you want something right away because you aren't satisfied with things the way they are. Can you see how easy it is when you are dissatisfied to make unwise decisions that can get you into debt? Yet, in most cases, if we just learn to wait, we can find ways to earn the money for what we want — just like you're doing for camp.

"There's a great story found in 2 Kings 4:1-7 about a widow with two sons who found a way to get out of debt with just a small jar of oil."

"A jar of oil?" Maria questioned. "Tell us about her."

"Long ago in Israel there was a young mother who was married to a prophet. They had two young sons. They borrowed some money, and sadly one day the father died before he could pay it back.

"In those days, if you could not repay a debt, you were sold as a slave. Soon after the father's death, the man who had loaned the money to them demanded that it be paid back. But the poor widow had no money, and her two boys were going to become slaves.

"The boys' mother was terribly upset. She had no way to earn enough money to pay the debt. But she knew a prophet named Elisha, and she went to ask him what she should do.

"Elisha was touched by this woman's story, so he asked, 'What do you have?'

"'I have nothing,' the mother answered, 'except a small jar of oil.'

"Elisha told her to collect as many empty jars and pots as she could from her neighbors. Then he instructed her, 'Take them to your house and pour the oil from your little jar into each empty pot and jar.'

"The woman hurried home and told her boys to help her gather all the containers they could find. When they had them in their house, they filled the jars just as Elisha had told her. The boys had never seen so much oil. The oil didn't stop flowing until all the jars were full!

"Elisha told her to sell the oil. Then he said, 'When you have the money, pay the man what you owe him. There will be enough money left for you to take care of your family.'

"The mother was very thankful, and the boys learned an important lesson about borrowing money. But they also learned that God loved them and would take care of them, as He did by multiplying the oil."

As Grandpa finished his story, he said, "God loves us and will take care of us. But we need to learn that borrowing money can sometimes lead to trouble.

"Today, when someone borrows money that person has to pay

interest on the money borrowed. Does anyone know what interest is?" Grandpa asked.

Ruth said, "I've heard my parents say that they have to pay a lot of interest on their debts, but I'm not sure what it is."

Grandpa explained, "When people borrow money, they have to pay back more than they actually borrowed. This extra money they have to pay is called interest. And interest can be very expensive. If you borrow a hundred dollars, you may have to pay as much as twenty dollars a year in interest until you pay it back."

Everyone moaned, and Grandpa continued. "Andy, think about that music club your brother suggested that you join. You will end up paying much more money than the CDs cost in the first place. You will worry about those debts all the time, wondering if you will ever get them paid. In that way you will be a servant to your brother and the music club until you pay them back."

As Grandpa talked, Andy squirmed, looking very uncomfortable. "I don't think I want to do that," he said. "I'm going to tell Eddie that I don't want to buy his CD player now. Instead I'm going to wait until I have enough money to pay cash for it."

"That's a very good decision, Andy," Grandpa said nodding.

"Now, let me give you the next clue to God's secret of handling money," Grandpa continued. "It is something you do, not something you have. Keep thinking about it. I know you'll discover the secret."

"We can hardly wait," Josh said.

They had no idea that a surprise was waiting for them early the next morning.

Memorize this scripture! *Just as the rich rule the poor, so the borrower is servant to the lender* (Proverbs 22:7, LB).

Answer these questions!

1. How does the dictionary define *debt*? _____
   _____
   _____

2. When someone pays interest on debt, what do you think that means?
   _____
   _____
   _____
   _____

3. Why do you think most people go into debt? _____
   _____
   _____
   _____
   _____

4. Read *Romans 13:8*. What does this verse say about owing money?
   _____
   _____
   _____

5. Read *Proverbs 22:7*. What does this verse say about someone who borrows money? _____
   _____
   _____
   _____

6. Why do you think the Lord wants us to stay out of debt?
   _____
   _____
   _____
   _____

Work it out!

List any money you owe and who loaned you the money. Then describe how you plan on paying it back.

Money I owe	Who loaned me the money	How I plan to pay it back
_____	_____	_____
_____	_____	_____
_____	_____	_____
_____	_____	_____

Get ready for the next chapter! Memorize *Proverbs 12:15* and answer the questions on pages 44 and 45.

Pray for me! Share your prayer requests with one another and write them down on the Prayer Lists. Then end the lesson by praying.

CHAPTER 5

The Big Day

The first rays of sunlight were just peeking over the horizon when the phone rang. Josh sleepily answered the phone and heard Grandpa's voice. "Josh, wake up! Abigail is about to have her babies. Get the kids and come over here!"

Andy had spent the night at Josh's house, so Josh whispered, "Andy, wake up!"

Andy pulled the pillow over his head and tried to go back to sleep, but Josh pulled the pillow away. "Andy, get up!" he said. "We've got to get over to Grandpa's right away because Abigail is having her babies."

That was all Andy needed. He jumped up and grabbed his clothes. Josh called Ruth and Maria. They met in front of Josh's house, and off they biked to Grandpa's.

Soon they were turning into Grandpa's driveway. They jumped off their bikes and heard Grandpa's voice calling to them from the barn, "Good morning. I was hoping you'd get here in time."

Just then a terrible squeal could be heard from Abigail's hut. "What's that awful noise?" asked Josh, eyes wide.

Grandpa said, "That's Abigail. It's time for her baby pigs to be born."

The kids started running to the hut. "Stop right there," Grandpa called in a stern voice. They stopped in surprise and looked at Grandpa.

"Listen carefully to me," he said. "You can help with the birth of Abigail's babies. But you must do exactly what I tell you. You won't be able to help if you cannot promise to follow my advice."

"Grandpa, we will do exactly what you say," said Josh.

"We sure will," Maria said. "Just tell us what to do."

Grandpa began giving them instructions. "Maria, run to Grandma and ask her to give you a pail of warm water, rubber gloves and some

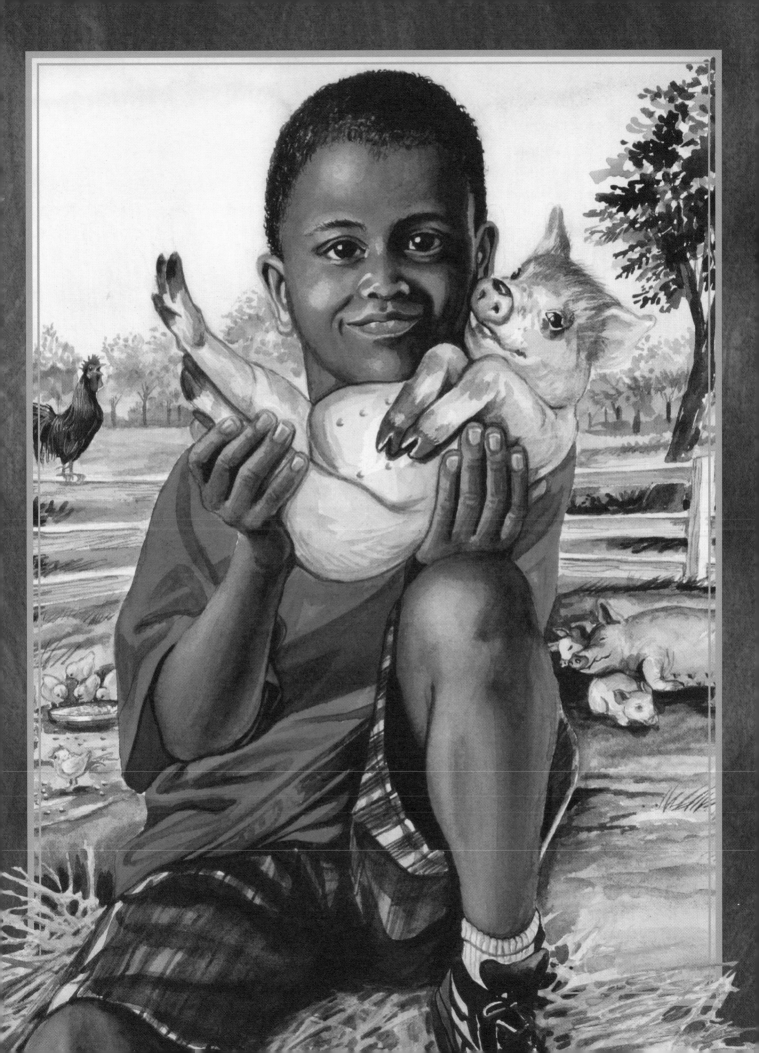

towels. Josh and Andy, break apart one of those bales of hay in the barn. You will need to hand me clean straw for each of the little pigs to lay on when it is born. Ruth, I will need you to keep wiping Abigail's head with warm water. Pigs have no sweat glands, and Abigail will get hot from her labor. It will make her feel better if you keep her head moistened with water."

By the time they arrived at Abigail's hut she lay on her side, grunting softly. Grandpa reached down and patted her belly. "Guess it's time, isn't it, girl?" he said in a soothing voice.

Just then Maria arrived with a pail of warm water and some towels. She handed Grandpa a pair of rubber gloves.

"What's that for?" asked Andy.

"So my hands will be clean when I touch Abigail's babies," replied Grandpa.

"How do you know what to do?" asked Maria.

"Well, God created Abigail to know just what to do," answered Grandpa. "All we'll do is to help her a little bit. Now all of you but Ruth just sit down over there on that bale of hay and watch. We don't want to make Abigail nervous."

As each little piglet was born, Grandpa wiped it off with warm water, then laid it on a fresh bed of straw that Josh and Andy handed to him. After about fifteen minutes, three little pink pigs lay on the straw near Abigail. As Grandpa wiped off the fourth little pig, he said, "Here, Andy. This looks like the last one. He's the littlest one too, the runt of the litter. How would you like to hold him?"

"Thanks!" said Andy, as Grandpa placed the little pig in his arms. "I'm the first one to hold one of Abigail's pigs." A great big smile spread across his face.

Abigail lay quietly, resting from her hard work. As Ruth wiped her head off one more time, she said, "Grandpa, what are we going to name the baby pigs?"

Grandpa smiled as he gently took the little pig from Andy's arms. He laid him on the straw by the others. The pigs squealed and began to crawl towards Abigail, tumbling over each other. "I have some ideas, Ruth," he responded. "But right now, Abigail needs to be alone with her babies. Let's go to the clubhouse and get cleaned up."

He pulled off his gloves. "I'm really proud of you," he said with a smile. "You listened to my advice and did just what I told you to do. You were great helpers!"

When they finished cleaning up, Grandpa said, "The way you listened to my advice would have made a king in the Bible very happy. His name was Solomon. He was the wisest man who ever lived, and he wrote most of the book of Proverbs. In today's lesson I want you to learn what Solomon said about seeking wise advice.

"Solomon told us that a wise person seeks counsel. Counsel is another word for advice. Proverbs 12:15 says, *The way of a fool is right in his own eyes, but a wise man is he who listens to counsel.*"

Grandpa pulled the little Bible out of his shirt pocket and continued. "Listen to these two verses from Proverbs and see if you can tell me why it is good to listen to counsel.

"Pride only breeds quarrels, but wisdom is found in those who take advice (13:10, NIV)."

"I know the answer to that one," said Ruth. "Listening to advice can help us to stay out of arguments and quarrels."

"That's right," said Grandpa. "Many people have money problems because they do not seek counsel. Now, how about this verse?

"Plans fail for lack of counsel, but with many advisors they succeed (15:22, NIV)."

"I know," Andy

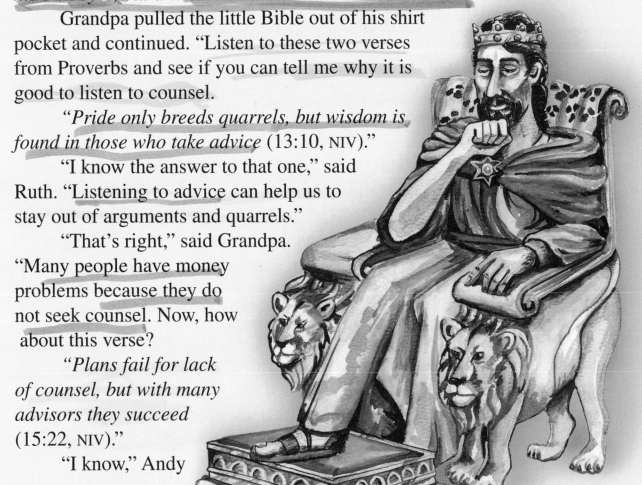

said. "Listening to advice will help us be successful when we are making plans."

"Like earning our way to baseball camp," added Josh. "Your advice is really helping us with that."

"That's right," said Grandpa. "Good advice gives you suggestions and ideas that will help you to make the right decisions. There are several places you can go to get good advice.

"The best advice is found in the Bible. Did you know that the Bible contains the very words of God? Maria, please look up 2 Timothy 3:16 and read it to us."

"Sure," Maria said reaching for the Bible. *"The whole Bible was given to us by inspiration from God and is useful to teach us what is true and to make us realize what is wrong in our lives; it straightens us out and helps us do what is right* (LB)."

"That's why it's so important for you to read the Bible every single day," said Grandpa. "It will keep you close to the Lord and give you answers to your problems.

"And the Bible also tells us to ask godly people for their advice. Listen to Psalm 37:30-31: *The godly man is a good counselor because he is just and fair and knows right from wrong* (LB)."

"My dad always has good advice for me," said Josh.

"You're right," continued Grandpa. "Our parents are a great source of counsel. Let me read what King Solomon said in Proverbs 6:20-22, *My son, observe the commandment of your father, and do not forsake the teaching of your mother; bind them continually on your heart; tie them around your neck. When you walk about, they will guide you; when you sleep, they will watch over you; and when you awake, they will talk to you.*

"Asking your parents' advice is a good way to honor them and will help build a close relationship with them. But we can also ask the Lord for His counsel when we pray. One of our Lord's names is Wonderful Counselor. Listen to what Psalm 32:8 has to say about the Lord's counsel. *I [the Lord] will instruct you and teach you in the way which you should go; I will counsel you with My eye upon you.*"

"Grandpa, what about fortune-tellers?" asked Andy.

"That's a good question," answered Grandpa. "The Bible tells us to never seek the advice of fortune-tellers, psychics or mediums. *Do not turn to mediums or spiritists; do not seek them out . . . I am the Lord your God* (Leviticus 19:31)."

"That means we should never read horoscopes or play with Ouija boards too, doesn't it?" asked Ruth.

"It sure does," said Grandpa. "Always stay away from them.

"We also need to avoid the advice of wicked people," Grandpa continued. "In fact, Psalm 1:1 tells us that we will be blessed if we do not seek advice from a wicked person.

"Well, it's time for another clue to help you discover God's secret to handling money. Are you trying to figure out the secret?"

"It's tough to figure out," said Ruth. "But so far we know that when we discover it it will mean even more to us than going to camp. And it is something we do and not have."

"That's exactly right, Ruth," said Grandpa. "Now let me give you another clue: You will find the answer in God's Word."

When he saw that they still did not have enough clues to guess it, he said, "Don't worry. Pretty soon the clues will lead you to the discovery."

"Grandpa," Josh said, "What do you think we should name the baby pigs?"

"Well," Grandpa said smiling, "There are four baby pigs and four of you. Each of you think up a name for one of them. And when we get together on Saturday, you can tell me."

"I already know what I want to name mine—the little runt," said Andy excitedly. "I'd like to call him Junior because he's so small and cute."

"And I'm going to call mine Babe," said Josh. "Babe Ruth was a big home run hitter and Babe's the biggest."

"Great names," said the others laughing. "Saturday will be a lot of fun."

Little did they know the trouble they were about to experience.

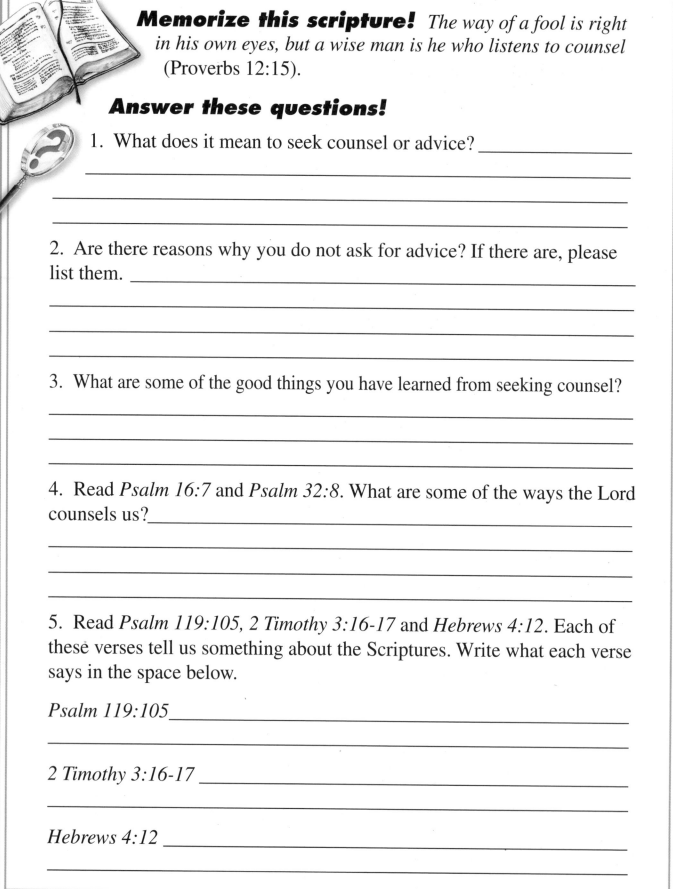

Memorize this scripture! *The way of a fool is right in his own eyes, but a wise man is he who listens to counsel* (Proverbs 12:15).

Answer these questions!

1. What does it mean to seek counsel or advice? _____
_____
_____
_____

2. Are there reasons why you do not ask for advice? If there are, please list them. _____
_____
_____
_____

3. What are some of the good things you have learned from seeking counsel?
_____
_____
_____

4. Read *Psalm 16:7* and *Psalm 32:8*. What are some of the ways the Lord counsels us?_____
_____
_____
_____

5. Read *Psalm 119:105, 2 Timothy 3:16-17* and *Hebrews 4:12*. Each of these verses tell us something about the Scriptures. Write what each verse says in the space below.

*Psalm 119:105*_____
_____

2 Timothy 3:16-17 _____
_____

Hebrews 4:12 _____
_____

6. Why do you think you should avoid the counsel of wicked people?

_____

_____

_____

Work it out!

Make a list of the people who will make good counselors for you,
and don't forget to put down your parents. Write down a
question to ask each of them about money. Then ask them!

Good counselor	Question to ask
_____	_____
	_____
	_____
_____	_____
	_____
	_____
_____	_____
	_____
	_____
_____	_____

Get ready for the next chapter! Memorize
Leviticus 19:11 and answer the questions on pages 53 and 54.

Pray for me! Share your prayer requests with one
another and write them down on the Prayer Lists.
Then end the lesson by praying.

CHAPTER 6

Honest in Small Things

*W*e had so much rain during the thunderstorm last night," said Coach Stevens, "the field is soaked. We're not going to be able to practice baseball today. I'll see you here tomorrow at the regular time for practice. Now remember, baseball camp is only three weeks away; we'll have a terrific time."

"And we're going," Andy whispered, winking at his friends.

"I've never seen so much lightning," said Maria shaking her head. "I couldn't get to sleep for hours."

"And what about all that thunder? It was so loud," said Josh.

"Let's go to Grandpa's," said Andy excitedly, "and see Junior and the rest of Abigail's babies." So off they pedaled.

When they arrived they saw Grandpa kneeling by Abigail's hut. His head was bowed and he wasn't moving. They ran over and Ruth asked excitedly, "How are Abigail's babies doing, Grandpa?"

When Grandpa raised his head, they knew something was terribly wrong. Tears streamed down his face.

The kids became silent. Finally Josh asked in a quiet voice, "What's wrong, Grandpa?"

"I came out to check on Abigail and her babies," answered Grandpa, "and Babe is missing."

They were shocked. Josh began to cry quietly, and Andy put his arm around him. "What could have happened to him?" Andy asked.

"One of three things," Grandpa replied. "A fox could have killed him; he could have wandered away; or someone could have stolen him."

"Stolen him!" Josh said with a touch of anger in his voice. "Who could have been so mean to do that?"

"Well, when I first came to town the local vet told me that some farm animals had been stolen in this area. And last night during the storm I heard Samson barking a lot. He could have been barking at a thief."

"What can we do?" Maria asked in a worried voice.

"I think we should pray," suggested Ruth.

"Good idea," answered Grandpa. "Remember what we learned in the second lesson—God is in control of everything. He knows exactly what happened to Babe and where he is. We're going to ask the Lord to protect Babe. And we're going to ask God to give us His wisdom on what we should do."

Everyone bowed their heads while Grandpa prayed. After he finished he said, "Now we need to search the field. If Babe wandered out of the hut, he's probably in the field. The grass is a little high, so Babe could be in it and we wouldn't see him."

They formed a straight line across. For an hour they walked back and forth from one end of the field to the other until they had walked over the whole field. But they didn't find him.

Grandpa finally said, "Let's go to the clubhouse."

The kids walked slowly to the clubhouse, sat on the hay and stared at the floor.

"I know you are discouraged, but this is a good time to learn the next lesson about God's ways of handling money," said Grandpa softly. "Maybe someone stole Babe because he didn't know that God wants us to always be honest. Josh, do you remember when the cashier gave you too much money when you checked out of the store and you were going to keep it? After we talked about it what did you do?"

"I returned the extra money to her," Josh answered. "And I remember you told me about the verse in Proverbs that says God hates dishonesty."

"That's right," said Grandpa with a smile. "Proverbs 20:23 says, *The Lord [hates] all cheating and dishonesty* (LB). Leviticus 19:11 says, *You shall not steal, nor deal falsely, nor lie to one another.*

"He wants us to be completely honest in every way, even with small things. Abraham in Genesis 14:22-23 is a wonderful example of a person who decided to be honest in small things. Listen to what he said, '*I have sworn to the Lord God Most High, possessor of heaven and earth, that I will not take a thread or a sandal thong or anything that is yours.*' Abraham promised God he wasn't even going to take something as small as a thread from someone else.

"Kids, have any of you ever

been dishonest?" Grandpa asked.

They were quiet. Finally Ruth said, "I took some candy from a store. I didn't feel good about it, but I didn't understand God wanted me to be so honest."

Then Andy said, "And I stole a CD from one of my brother's friends."

Maria blushed and said, "And I haven't been honest during some of my math tests. I have such a hard time with that class."

Grandpa beamed. "I am so proud that you were brave enough to tell me these things. Let's look more closely at what the Lord says about honesty, and maybe you will want to make a promise like Abraham."

He opened his Bible to Romans 13:9-10 and read, *"If you love your neighbor as much as you love yourself you will not want to harm or cheat him . . . or steal from him . . . love does no wrong to anyone* (LB)." Grandpa continued, "Any time we're dishonest, we hurt another person — just the way we are hurting now because someone may have stolen Babe.

"Let's look at Daniel, one of my favorite people in the Bible. His life can also help us understand why it is important to be honest.

"As a young boy, Daniel was taken captive to live in Babylon after his country was defeated in war. But even though he was in a strange new land, Daniel decided to be honest always. The king recognized his honesty, so he asked Daniel to serve in his palace.

"When Daniel had become an old man, a new king named Darius decided to make Daniel the chief ruler of his kingdom.

"This made some evil people very jealous. They watched him carefully to see if he was doing anything dishonestly so they could tell the king. But Daniel was always honest.

"Finally, these evil men thought of a plan to kill Daniel. They went to the king and asked him to make a law that no one could pray to anyone except King Darius for 30 days. If anyone broke

50

this law, they were to be thrown into a den of lions.

"Even though Daniel knew about the law, he still knelt and prayed to God three times every day. When the evil men discovered that Daniel had broken the law, they told the king.

"At last Darius understood why the evil men had suggested such a law. Even though he liked Daniel, he had no choice but to throw him into the lion's den. Then, with a heavy heart he returned to his palace, unable to sleep all night.

"With the first light of dawn, the king hurried to the den, and cried out, '*Daniel, servant of the living God, has your God, whom you serve continually, been able to rescue you from the lions?*'

"Daniel answered, '*O king, live forever! My God sent his angel, and he shut the mouths of the lions . . . because I was found innocent*' (Daniel 6:20-22, NIV). You see, when we are honest, it pleases the Lord."

"What should we do if we've already been dishonest?" Ruth asked sheepishly.

"God teaches us to return anything we have taken that doesn't belong to us," Grandpa said. "In fact, the Bible tells us that if we get anything dishonestly, we must return it to its owner with something extra — this is called restitution. Restitution is a way to say, 'I am sorry. Please forgive me.' In the New Testament, Zaccheus gave us a good example of restitution. Andy, read what he said in Luke 19:8."

"*If I have cheated anybody out of anything, I will pay back four times the amount* (NIV)," read Andy.

"Honesty and restitution are hard because so many people around us are dishonest," said Grandpa.

Suddenly Josh jumped up, shouting, "Did you hear that noise?" He tripped over the bale of hay he was sitting on as he ran over to the corner of the barn where Samson slept at night. There, a lost and hungry baby pig was snuggling up to Samson. "He's here!" Josh shouted. "Babe's here!"

Everyone happily ran over to see. "I think I know what must have happened," Grandpa said with a grin. "Babe became frightened by the thunderstorm and ran out of the hut. Samson saw him wandering around and guided him safely to the barn by barking. Come on, Josh, carry Babe to Abigail. Then I want to find out what the rest of you have decided to name your baby pigs."

Never had they heard such happy squealing as when Abigail and her lost baby were reunited.

"Well, tell me the names of your baby pigs," said Grandpa after Abigail and Babe had quieted down.

"I'd like to call mine Eve," said Ruth, "because she was the first girl born."

"And the name of my baby pig will be Hope," said Maria, "since I hope we can go to camp."

"Those are great names," said Grandpa, smiling. "How much money do you have saved toward camp?"

"We have almost half the money we need," replied Ruth. "But we only have three weeks left. When are we going to finish fixing the fence so you can bring the horses for us to take care of and earn some more money?"

"Next week," said Grandpa. "This Saturday I need your help with something else. We are going to give free rabies shots to pets down at the animal clinic for people who can't afford to pay for the shots. A lot of people and pets will come, and I'll need your help to keep things running smoothly. But the clinic can't afford to pay anyone, so you will have to volunteer your time."

"That's all right," said Maria. "I remember seeing a program that showed how terrible rabies can be." The rest quickly agreed.

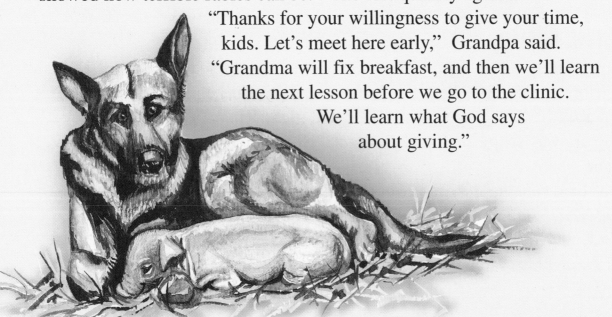

"Thanks for your willingness to give your time, kids. Let's meet here early," Grandpa said. "Grandma will fix breakfast, and then we'll learn the next lesson before we go to the clinic. We'll learn what God says about giving."

Memorize this scripture! *You shall not steal, nor deal falsely, nor lie to one another* (Leviticus 19:11).

Answer these questions!

1. Read *Leviticus 19:11* and *Exodus 20:15*. According to these verses, what does the Lord say about being honest?

_____

_____

2. Look up *Luke 16:10*. Why do you think Jesus said we should be honest in small things? _____

_____

_____

3. Are you always honest —even in small things? _____

_____

_____

_____

4. If you are not always honest, what will you do to change?

_____

_____

_____

5. Look up the word *restitution* in the dictionary. How would you define it?

_____

_____

_____

6. What should you do if you took something dishonestly?

_____

_____

_____

7. What was the most important thing you learned from reading this chapter?

_____

_____

_____

_____

Work it out!

Make a list of the things you would like to buy. Write down how much they will cost and how you plan on saving enough to buy them.

What I want to buy	How much it will cost	How I will save
_____	_____	_____
		_____
_____	_____	_____
		_____
_____	_____	_____
		_____
_____	_____	_____
		_____
_____	_____	_____
		_____

Get ready for the next chapter! Memorize *Acts 20:35* and answer the questions on pages 62 and 63.

Pray for me! Share your prayer requests with one another and write them down on the Prayer Lists. Then end the lesson by praying.

CHAPTER 7

Midnight

Even before the kids reached the kitchen, they could smell the delicious pancakes.

"Come on in," said Grandpa. "I hope you brought your appetites, because you're going to love Grandma's breakfast."

"Boy, are we hungry," exclaimed Andy as the kids eagerly sat around the table.

After Grandpa prayed, thanking the Lord for breakfast, they started eating. When they finished Grandpa took out his Bible and said, "As you know, we're giving free rabies shots at the clinic this morning. There are going to be a lot of people there with their pets. Your job will be to make sure I have a record of every animal that gets a shot.

"You are giving your time to help others, and I really appreciate it," Grandpa said smiling. "I also appreciate your great attitude."

Grandpa continued, "Having the right attitude when we give money also is important. Josh, look up 1 Corinthians 13:3. Read it and tell us what you think it says about our attitude."

Josh read, *"If I give all my possessions to feed the poor . . . but do not have love, it profits me nothing.* I've never thought about this before," said Josh with a puzzled expression on his face. "It says even if I gave everything away, but did it without love, it wouldn't do me any good."

"You're right," said Grandpa nodding. "Maria, will you please read 2 Corinthians 9:7?"

"Sure," said Maria. *"God loves a cheerful giver."*

"But how can we always give with love and be cheerful?" asked Ruth. "Sometimes I just don't want to give, especially when I'm working hard to save money for something I really want -- like going to camp."

"That's a good question," Grandpa answered. "If you kids don't

remember anything else about giving, remember this. You should give every gift just as if you are giving to Jesus — even though it is going to be used to help others. And we can be loving and cheerful when we do that. Giving to the Lord is one way to thank Him for making us, loving us, providing food for us, and for dying on a cross so that our sins can be forgiven."

"I'd never thought about that," Josh spoke up suddenly. "Grandpa, there's a verse in the Bible that says something about giving instead of receiving, isn't there?"

"You're thinking of Acts 20:35," said Grandpa. "It says, *Remember the words of the Lord Jesus, that He Himself said, 'It is more blessed to give than to receive.'*"

"What!" exclaimed Andy in disbelief. "Are you sure about that? How can it be better to give than to receive? That doesn't sound right to me."

"I understand, Andy," said Grandpa smiling. "I didn't believe it either the first time I heard this truth, because we all know how good it feels to receive a gift. But when you start giving, you'll find out that it really is a bigger blessing to give than to receive."

"Just how much of our money does God want us to give away?" asked Andy with a worried look on his face.

"Well, Andy, why don't you read Malachi 3:8-9 for us," Grandpa responded.

"Sure," Andy said reaching for the Bible. "*Will a man rob God? Yet you are robbing Me! But you say, 'How have we robbed Thee?' In tithes and offerings. You are cursed with a curse, for you are robbing Me.*

"This is a little hard to understand," Andy said. "It says something about tithes and robbing God. What's a tithe?"

"A tithe is ten percent of the money you receive," Grandpa answered. "If you earn a dollar, a tithe would be ten cents. In the Old Testament God commanded His

58

people to give a tithe. If they didn't, it was the same thing as robbing Him."

"So if we tithe, that's all we have to give?" asked Josh.

Grandpa smiled, "I think the best way to answer you is to tell you a Bible story about a woman who gave everything that she had. One day, Jesus and His disciples were visiting the temple in Jerusalem. Jesus watched a poor widow wearing tattered clothing come into the temple. Although she was poor, her face was radiant because she was so joyful.

"As she passed the box where people gave their money, she took two small copper coins that were worth less than a penny and dropped them into the box.

"Listen to what Jesus told His disciples. '*This poor widow put in more than all the contributors to the treasury; for they all put in out of their surplus, but she, out of her poverty*' (Mark 12:43-44)."

Andy interrupted Grandpa's story with a question. "But Grandpa," he asked, "how could she buy food?"

"Remember what we learned in the lesson about God's part?" answered Grandpa. "He is the One who provides for our needs. The poor widow was trusting the Lord to give her what she needed to live on."

By the time Grandpa finished his story, it was time to go. "Well," he said, "now we've got to leave for the clinic. When we've finished our work there, I'll tell you a couple more things about giving."

When they arrived at the clinic, the parking lot was already filled with people and animals. There were dogs, cats, rabbits, goats and even a couple of raccoons. It looked like a little zoo!

"Josh and Andy, help the people make two straight lines leading up to the doors," said Grandpa, pointing to two side doors. "Maria and Ruth, come inside with me. I want you to get two clipboards with information cards. You can give a card to every person in line to fill out. That way we'll get their names and addresses along with the name and description of every pet."

They worked hard all morning. By the time Grandpa gave the last shot, the kids were ready for a break.

Just then an old blue pickup truck pulled up. A tiny, older woman dressed in blue jeans and a sweatshirt called out, "Doc! I need you to come over here and give me a hand."

"Who is that?" Josh asked.

"That's Mrs. Nichols," he explained. "She loves animals and picks up all the strays she finds. Come on, let's see what she wants."

They walked over to her pickup truck, and in the back lay a tiny black lamb whose leg was badly hurt. As Grandpa started examining the lamb, Mrs. Nichols explained.

"I found her by the side of the road out in the country," she said. "I stopped at the nearby houses but no one knew anything about her. I think someone must have just left her there because they didn't want her. I fed her with a baby bottle, but I can't afford to keep her."

"Oh, she's so cute!" said Maria.

Grandpa checked the lamb's leg carefully and said, "Her leg is broken and she will need a splint on it so it can heal."

Then Andy leaned over and asked, "May I hold her?"

"Sure," Grandpa said as he laid the lamb carefully in Andy's arms. "We'll put the splint on her broken leg and then decide what to do with her."

Slowly Andy carried the little lamb to the clinic. There Grandpa skillfully fitted a splint on her leg.

"I've got an idea," Andy suddenly said. "Grandpa, why don't we take her to your farm? I'll do some extra work to earn enough money to pay for her food."

"Andy, that's wonderful," Grandpa said smiling. "I think you're beginning to understand what Jesus meant when He said it is more blessed to give than to receive."

"I see what you mean," Andy said, petting the lamb. "May I name the lamb Midnight?"

"That's a great name," Grandpa answered as he put the last instruments in his old black vet bag.

Then Maria spoke up, "Grandpa, you said you were going to tell us something else about giving."

"Thanks for reminding me. Does anyone want to guess who the Lord wants us to give to?" he asked.

"It's important to give to your church," said Ruth.

"And to those who are poor," added Josh.

"You're right," said Grandpa. "You might be surprised to learn that when we give to help a poor person, we are actually giving to Jesus Christ." Grandpa pulled out his Bible. "Let me read Matthew 25:37-40, *Then the righteous will answer Him, saying, 'Lord, when did we see You hungry, and feed You, or thirsty, and give you drink?' . . . The King will answer and say to them, 'Truly I say to you, to the extent that you did it to one of these brothers of Mine, even the least of them, you did it to Me.'*

"God approves of your working to earn and save money for camp. But you should also give some of what you earn to others who need it."

"Maybe we could pray that God will show us someone who needs something that we could give," suggested Ruth.

"And maybe that person could help you discover God's secret to handling money," said Grandpa.

"That's another clue, isn't it?" said Andy. "I like that idea. Let's pray right now!"

Grandpa and the four kids bowed their heads. One by one, each prayed for God to show them someone who needed something that they could give. It was a prayer that the Lord was going to answer in a very unexpected way.

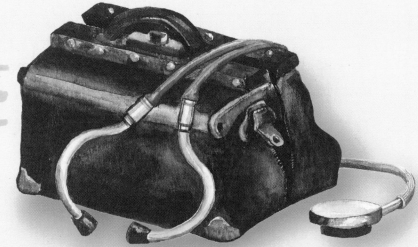

61

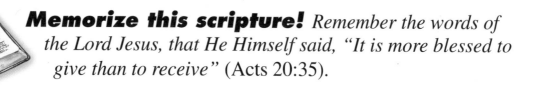

Memorize this scripture! *Remember the words of the Lord Jesus, that He Himself said, "It is more blessed to give than to receive" (Acts 20:35).*

Answer these questions!

1. The Lord says it is important to give with the right attitude. Look up 1 *Corinthians 13:3* and *2 Corinthians 9:7*. According to these verses, what attitudes should we have when we give?

1 Corinthians 13:3 _____

_____

_____

2 Corinthians 9:7 _____

_____

_____

2. How do you think you can learn to give cheerfully and from a heart filled with love? _____

_____

_____

3. Do you think it is better to give a gift or receive a gift? Why?

_____

_____

_____

Look up *Acts 20:35*. How do think the Lord would answer this question?

_____

_____

4. List the benefits to the giver found in *Proverbs 11:24-25* and *Matthew 6:20*.
Proverbs 11:24-25 _____

_____

Matthew 6:20 _____

_____

5. Look up the word *tithe* in the dictionary. What does it mean to tithe?

_____

_____

6. How much of your income do you give? _____

_____

7. Do you think it is important to give to your church? Why?

_____

_____

8. Look up *Proverbs 28:27* and *Matthew 25:34-45*. What do these passages say about giving to the poor?

Proverbs 28:27 _____

_____

Matthew 25:34 -45 _____

_____

Work it out! Begin to pray for the Lord to bring someone into your life whom you can help by giving. Then make a list of those whom you want to give to and write down how much you would like to give . . . don't forget your church.

Who I want to give to   How much I want to give

_____   _____

_____   _____

_____   _____

_____   _____

Get ready for the next chapter! Memorize *Colossians 3:23-24* and answer the questions on pages 70 and 71.

Pray for me! Share your prayer requests with one another and write them down on the Prayer Lists. Then end the lesson by praying.

CHAPTER 8

Just Like Nehemiah

G randpa," said Josh over the phone. "May we ask our parents if we can bring our sleeping bags and camp out in the clubhouse tonight? That way we can start working on the fence early tomorrow."

"And that way you can see Babe and Midnight," Grandpa laughed. "I'll let you do it if you kids come early enough to roast some hot dogs over a fire. And I'll sleep on my old army cot out in the barn."

"That would be fun!" Josh exclaimed.

After the kids got permission to spend the night, they picked up their sleeping bags. Then they hurried over to the barn and arrived just as Grandpa was starting the fire.

"Why don't you put your sleeping bags out in the clubhouse?" Grandpa called out. "Then you boys can check on the baby pigs and Midnight. Maria and Ruth, you can help Grandma get the hot dogs ready. She's also fixing some fresh ears of corn for us to roast."

Soon they were sitting around the fire eating hot dogs and corn. They talked about the animals and about all the different things they had been doing to earn money for baseball camp.

"Remember all those jobs we thought about doing?" said Josh. "Well, we've done most of them, and we have almost enough money to go to camp. God has really helped us."

"I know God is pleased with the way you have worked hard and learned how to handle money well," said Grandpa with a big smile.

"It's all because you started teaching us about God's way to handle money," said Ruth.

After supper they roasted marshmallows and sang songs around the

fire. Finally Grandpa said, "It's time to get some sleep so we can finish the fence tomorrow."

"Grandpa," Andy asked. "Do you think it would be all right if Midnight slept next to me? She must be lonely."

"Andy, I think that's a good idea. And Josh, you can go get Babe if you want him to sleep next to you," Grandpa said with a big grin.

The boys ran to get Midnight and Babe. Then everyone went into the clubhouse and spread their sleeping bags out on the thick pile of straw that Grandpa had laid on the floor. Just as he was about to close the door, Samson and Patches hurried inside.

"It's time for us to go to sleep. We have to get up early tomorrow to work on the fence," said Grandpa, sitting down on his cot.

"Will you tell us a story first?" asked Ruth.

Grandpa nodded. "After we finish the fence tomorrow, we're going to learn what God says about work. So let me tell you a story about a man in the Bible who built a fence. Well, actually it was a wall around an entire city. His name was Nehemiah. He lived during a time when some of God's people were returning to their home town of Jerusalem after years of captivity in a faraway land. Nehemiah can teach us some things about work."

The kids curled up in their sleeping bags and listened carefully. "Nehemiah worked for the king who captured Jerusalem. One day Nehemiah heard bad news. The wall around Jerusalem was torn down. Those who lived in the city were poor and could not get the materials to rebuild the wall. Because the city had no walls, their enemies could attack them any time they wanted.

"Nehemiah's heart was broken by this news. He longed to see Jerusalem become a safe city. He prayed for the Lord to allow him to go and help build the wall. After he had prayed for several months, he told the king about the broken wall in Jerusalem.

"God worked in the king's heart, and he agreed to let Nehemiah go. The king even gave him supplies to build the wall.

"Nehemiah was very thankful. After he made the long journey, he met with the people of Jerusalem to tell them about his plan to fix the wall. He explained that God had caused the king to let him come to rebuild the wall. When he finished, the people said, 'Let us build the wall.'

"The people began to build the new wall. But their enemies heard about this and decided to stop their work. First they sent people to make fun of the workers. When this didn't stop them, they decided to kill the workers.

"But Nehemiah heard about their plan and was ready with a better plan. He told half of the workers to work on the wall, and he gave swords to the other half to protect them as they worked. Day and night the guards watched for the enemies' attack.

"Try as they might, the enemies could not stop Nehemiah and the workers from building the wall. After only 52 days the wall was completed. God had really helped them."

As Grandpa finished his story, Andy said sleepily, "That's what the Lord is doing for us, isn't it? He is helping us so that we can go to camp."

"That's right," said Grandpa. He looked around with a smile at his band of workers. Josh's arm was draped over Babe's side. Patches was curled up next to Maria. Samson lay at Ruth's feet.

Sleepily Andy spoke up. "Good night, Grandpa. This worker is going to sleep so I can help build the fence tomorrow," he said, pulling Midnight closer.

❊   ❊   ❊

They were awakened at the crack of dawn when the rooster started crowing. Grandma was already in the kitchen preparing a hearty breakfast of scrambled eggs and homemade blueberry muffins. After breakfast they started on the fence and completely finished it before lunch.

"You all did a great job," Grandpa said, his face beaming. "Nehemiah would have been happy to have you working with him on the wall around Jerusalem. Let's go back to the clubhouse and talk about what God wants us to know about work."

When they got settled in the clubhouse, Grandpa began. "Work is so important that 2 Thessalonians 3:10 says, *If anyone will not work, neither let him eat.* You see, one of the reasons God knows you should work is because work helps you grow and it builds your character. For example, while you were building the fence, the fence was also building you. It improved your skill in using a hammer, made you more diligent and even helped your muscles grow stronger.

"Does it surprise you to learn that God plays a big part in our work?" Grandpa asked. "First, God gives each of us special skills and abilities. Exodus 36:1 tells us, *And every skillful person in whom the Lord has put skill.* God has given each of you special talents.

"Ruth, you have a wonderful talent for music. Andy, you are a gifted baseball player. It is not a matter of one person being better than someone else. It is simply a matter of having received different abilities."

"Grandpa, how else does God help us in our work?" Josh asked.

"God is the one who gives success," answered Grandpa as he took out his Bible. "Ruth, read what Genesis 39:2-3 says about Joseph."

Ruth read, *"The Lord was with Joseph, so he became a successful man . . . his master saw that the Lord was with him and how the Lord caused all that he did to prosper in his hand.* So God has been helping us as we have worked to get our money for camp."

"That's right, Ruth," said Grandpa. And there

is one other thing the Bible tells us. We should do our work for the Lord. *Whatever you do, do your work heartily, as for the Lord rather than for men . . . It is the Lord Christ whom you serve* (Colossians 3:23-24).

"Think about your attitude toward work or school. If you could see Jesus as your boss or teacher, would you have a better attitude or try to work harder? I know that sometimes when I forget I am working for Christ, I don't do as good a job," said Grandpa.

"The Bible encourages hard work. Wise King Solomon wrote in Ecclesiastes 9:10, *Whatever your hand finds to do . . . do it with all your might.* The next time you come over you're going to meet some small creatures who are both hard workers and wise savers. And that will be the next lesson — learning what God says about saving."

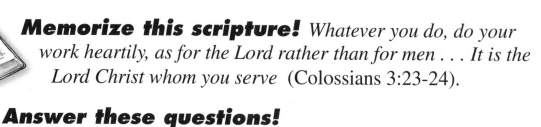

Memorize this scripture! *Whatever you do, do your work heartily, as for the Lord rather than for men . . . It is the Lord Christ whom you serve* (Colossians 3:23-24).

Answer these questions!

1. God plays a role in your work. Look up *Genesis 39:2-5, Exodus 36:1-2* and *Psalm 75:6-7*. What do each of these verses tell you about how the Lord is involved in work?

Genesis 39:2-5 _____

_____

_____

Exodus 36:1-2 _____

_____

_____

Psalm 75:6-7 _____

_____

_____

2. Do you think most people understand the Lord is so involved in their work? Why? _____

_____

_____

3. Read *Proverbs 6:6-11* and *2 Thessalonians 3:7-10*. What do these passages say about working hard?

Proverbs 6:6-11 _____

_____

_____

2 Thessalonians 3:7-10 _____

_____

_____

4. Do you work hard at home and school? If you don't, what will you do to change? _____

_____

_____

5. Carefully study *Colossians 3:22-25*. Whom do you really work for? Now that you understand this truth, how will it change your work habits?

_____

_____

Work it out!

Think about some jobs that are done by eight-to-twelve-year-olds.

❏ Washing cars   ❏ Household chores

❏ Raking leaves   ❏ Shoveling snow

❏ Feeding pets   ❏ Babysitting

❏ Mowing lawns   ❏ Yard work

❏ Walking dogs   ❏ Paper routes

Write down a list of jobs you could do to earn money. Then try to get a job this week.

Jobs I might be able to do

1. _____

2. _____

3. _____

4. _____

What do you think you should say and how should you act and dress when you go ask for a job?_____

_____

_____

Get ready for the next chapter!

Memorize *Proverbs 21:20* and *Proverbs 21:5* and answer the questions on pages 78 and 79.

Pray for me! Share your prayer requests with one another and write them down on the Prayer Lists. Then end the lesson by praying.

Small but Wise

When the four friends arrived at Grandpa's house, he was on the porch bending over a table that had a green box on it. When he saw them getting off their bikes, he called out, "You're just in time."

"Just in time for what, Grandpa?" asked Josh.

"Just in time to help me with our ant farm," said Grandpa.

"Ant farm!" Andy and Maria exclaimed at the same time.

"What are you going to do with ants?" asked Andy.

"Ants can teach us something about saving, Andy," Grandpa answered. They gathered around the table to take a closer look at the box. It was about two feet tall and two feet wide. But it was only a few inches thick. One side of the box was made of glass.

"Look at this," Andy said, his eyes flashing with excitement.

The ants scurried up and down little tunnels leading from the top of the dirt in the box all the way to the bottom. Several rounded out little "rooms" could be seen.

Grandpa continued. "The ants feed the queen, take care of her babies, look for food and build the tunnels. The queen stays in her room making eggs for new ants."

"Look at the way they carry the bread crumbs from the top of the ground down into the little rooms below," said Maria. "They save a lot of food, don't they?"

"Yes," Grandpa answered. "Some food will be eaten right away, but some food they save to eat another day.

"Listen to what the Bible tells us about the ants. *Four things on earth are small, yet they are extremely wise: ants are creatures of little strength, yet they store up their food in the summer* (Proverbs 30:24-25, NIV)."

"They do that so they will have food to eat during winter when they cannot find any food on the ground, right, Grandpa?" Josh asked.

"That's right. And just like those wise ants, we should save too. But instead of food we need to save some of our money each time we receive some. Proverbs 21:20 says, *The wise man saves for the future, but the foolish man spends whatever he gets* (LB). When we save we will have money when we need to buy something in the future. It also helps us stay out of debt.

"It's a good time for each of you to open a savings account at a bank. Then when you receive money, you can put some of it in the bank. When you put your savings into the bank," Grandpa continued, "it actually grows, and you end up with more money than you put in. This extra money is called interest. Every month that you leave your money in the bank, the bank adds the interest to the total that you have. The longer you leave your money in the bank, the more interest you earn.

"And if you are always faithful to save, your savings and the interest that you earn can grow into a lot of money. Wise King Solomon wrote, *Steady plodding brings prosperity* (Proverbs 21:5, LB). 'Plodding' means to keep doing something over and over again. If you will be a regular saver, the amount of money you have will grow to become large."

"But, Grandpa," said Josh. "I've seen advertisements on television that said if I gambled or played the lottery, I could become rich. Is that true?"

"Good question, Josh," answered Grandpa shaking his head sadly. "A lot of people gamble, and many of them do it to make money fast without having to work. This does not please the Lord. Unfortunately, most people lose money when they gamble. And many people can't stop gambling once they start. Some of them even gamble away the money that is needed to buy food for their family. Grandma and I have decided it is best never to gamble — even a penny."

"Saving is a lot wiser than gambling, isn't it, Grandpa?" said Maria.

"It sure is," replied Grandpa. "The Bible tells about a young man who saved a whole country from starving because he learned how to save.

"The man's name was Joseph. He came from a big family of eleven brothers. Joseph was his father's favorite son. His father made a beautiful, colorful coat for Joseph. Joseph's brothers became so jealous of him they decided to get rid of him. So they stripped off his coat, threw him into a pit, and left him to die. But later they sold him to some people traveling to Egypt. To cover up what they had done, the brothers tore Joseph's coat and told their father that he had been killed by a wild animal.

"When Joseph arrived in Egypt, he was sold as a slave to one of the men who worked for Pharaoh, the king. Later this man's wife lied about Joseph and he was thrown in prison. He stayed in prison for seven long years.

"One day Pharaoh had a disturbing dream, but no one could tell him the meaning of it. One of Pharaoh's men remembered that Joseph had interpreted his dream, and they sent for Joseph to interpret Pharaoh's dream.

"With God's help, Joseph was able to interpret Pharaoh's dream. The dream told about seven years when there would be plenty of food in Egypt. At the end of the seven years, a famine would begin and would last for seven more years, during which there would be no food.

"Pharaoh was so thankful to Joseph for interpreting his dream that he made him the ruler over the land of Egypt.

"Joseph ordered everyone to save and store some of their food in Pharaoh's buildings so there would be enough food when the famine began. When the famine began, he sold the food to feed the people during the time when no food would grow.

"The terrible famine spread to all the nearby countries. Hungry and starving, Joseph's brothers came to Egypt for food. Joseph recognized them at once, but they did not recognize him. He sold them food, and later he told them who he was. His brothers were shocked to see him, and they were sorry for what they had done. Joseph forgave his brothers and asked them to bring his father and their families to Egypt to live."

The children had listened carefully to Grandpa's story, but now Josh interrupted. "I wouldn't forgive them. They threw him in a pit and tried to kill him. I would let them starve."

"Joseph never forgot what his brothers did to him. But he also never forgot how God had taken care of him and allowed him to become a great ruler. He forgave his brothers because he loved them, and because he knew God had sent him to Egypt to save his family's lives."

"But," said Maria, a look of great sadness on her face, "they really hurt him. It's hard to forgive people that really hurt you."

Grandpa looked at each child. "That's true, Maria. It is hard. But Joseph is a picture of someone else in the Bible who was hurt deeply by the people He loved."

"You mean Jesus, don't you?" Ruth said softly.

"Yes, Ruth," Grandpa continued. "God loves us. In fact, He loves us so much that He sent His only Son, Jesus, to earth to die for us. John 3:16 says, *For God so loved the world that He gave His only begotten Son, that whoever believes in Him should not perish, but have eternal life.*

"God wants us to know Him and become part of His wonderful family. Unfortunately, each of us is separated from God because of sin. God is holy — which means He is perfect. But all of us have sinned. That means we have done wrong things like disobeying our parents or saying unkind words to someone. Romans 3:23 reads, *For all have sinned and fall short of the glory of God.*

"Jesus came to die, be buried and rise again so He could take away our sins. He did this so we could become members of God's family. Jesus said, *'I am the way, and the truth, and the life; no one comes to the Father, but through Me'* (John 14:6). Jesus is the only way to heaven.

"We all need to ask Jesus to come into our hearts. When we do that, God will forgive our sins and allow us to live with Him in heaven forever. It is the most important thing you will ever do in your life."

"I've asked Jesus to be my Savior and to take away all my sins," said Josh.

"Me, too," said Ruth. "My parents told me about Jesus and prayed with me and I asked Him to forgive my sins."

"Grandpa Pete," said Andy, his beautiful, dark eyes brimming with tears. "I've never asked Jesus to come into my heart and to forgive me for all the wrong things I've done. What do I need to do?"

"Me, either," added Maria. "How can I come to Jesus?"

"All you need to do is pray," said Grandpa. "In fact, let's pray right now. All of you bow your heads and repeat the words I pray."

They bowed their heads and prayed. "Dear Father, thank You for sending Your Son, Jesus Christ, to die on the cross for my sins. Thank You for loving me so much. Please forgive me of all my sins and come into my heart and become my Savior. I really want You as my Savior from sin. Thank You for coming into my heart, dear Lord. Amen."

As they lifted their heads, Maria said, "Grandpa, thank you so much for introducing Andy and me to Jesus. But Grandpa, now I want God to answer our prayer and bring someone into our lives that we can give something to. When is God going to answer that prayer?"

"I don't know when He will answer that prayer, Maria," answered Grandpa. "But I don't think it will be too much longer. Guess what?" Grandpa exclaimed. "Next Saturday the horses will be here. I've also invited a special friend to join us. I think she'll become a special friend of yours, too."

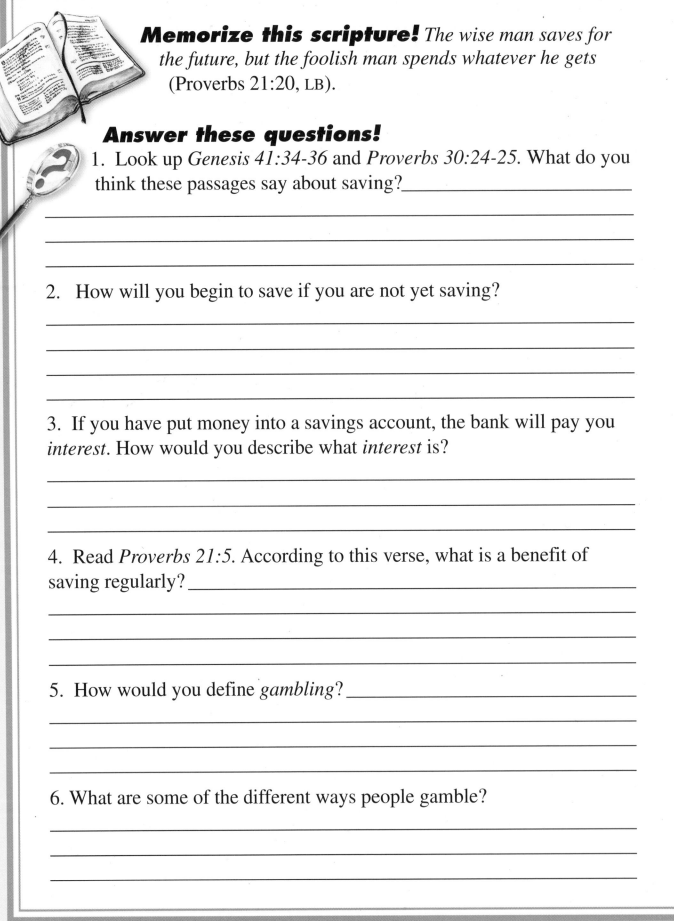

Memorize this scripture! *The wise man saves for the future, but the foolish man spends whatever he gets* (Proverbs 21:20, LB).

Answer these questions!

1. Look up *Genesis 41:34-36* and *Proverbs 30:24-25*. What do you think these passages say about saving?_____
_____
_____
_____

2. How will you begin to save if you are not yet saving?
_____
_____
_____
_____

3. If you have put money into a savings account, the bank will pay you *interest*. How would you describe what *interest* is?
_____
_____
_____

4. Read *Proverbs 21:5*. According to this verse, what is a benefit of saving regularly? _____
_____
_____
_____

5. How would you define *gambling*? _____
_____
_____
_____

6. What are some of the different ways people gamble?
_____
_____
_____

7. Why do you think most people gamble? _____

_____

_____

_____

8. Do you think gambling pleases the Lord? Why?

_____

_____

_____

Work it out!

   If you do not have a savings account, open one. Ask the person who opens the account how much interest they will pay you on your savings. Write down the interest rate you will be paid: _____%.

Did you ask Jesus to come into your heart and forgive your sins?
If you did, be sure to tell your teacher or parents so they can
help you grow to know the Lord better.

Get ready for the next chapter!
   Memorize *1 Timothy 4:12* and answer the questions on pages 86 and 87.

   Pray for me! Share your prayer requests with one another and write them down on the Prayer Lists. Then end the lesson by praying.

Friends

The kids were just starting their chores when they heard someone turning into the driveway. They rushed out in time to see Grandpa driving his truck and hauling a trailer. The tails of two horses stuck out the back of the trailer, blowing in the wind.

"Let's go see the horses!" shouted Josh excitedly as he ran toward the truck.

"Good morning," said Grandpa cheerfully. "You're about to meet two great horses. You'll need to stay calm, though, so they can get used to you."

He opened the trailer door and led the first horse out. It was a large, handsome reddish-brown colored horse. "Her name is Cinnamon," said Grandpa as he petted her nose gently. "And she is the pony's mom. Josh, hold the rope tied to her bridle while I get the pony out of the trailer."

The pony was the color of honey. He was feisty and had flashing eyes.

"Oh, he's beautiful," said Ruth. "What's his name?"

"Shooting Star," replied Grandpa. "The night he was born, Grandma and I saw a shooting star. We thought it would be just the name for him. Let's walk them to the field. We'll leave them alone for a while so they can get used to their new home."

After he closed the gate Grandpa said, "Let's go to the clubhouse and talk about the next lesson."

After everyone had taken out their Bible Grandpa asked, "Do you know the Lord said that choosing the right kind of close friends is important? Close friends either help or hurt our walk with the Lord. Maria, read 1 Corinthians 15:33 and tell us what you think it means."

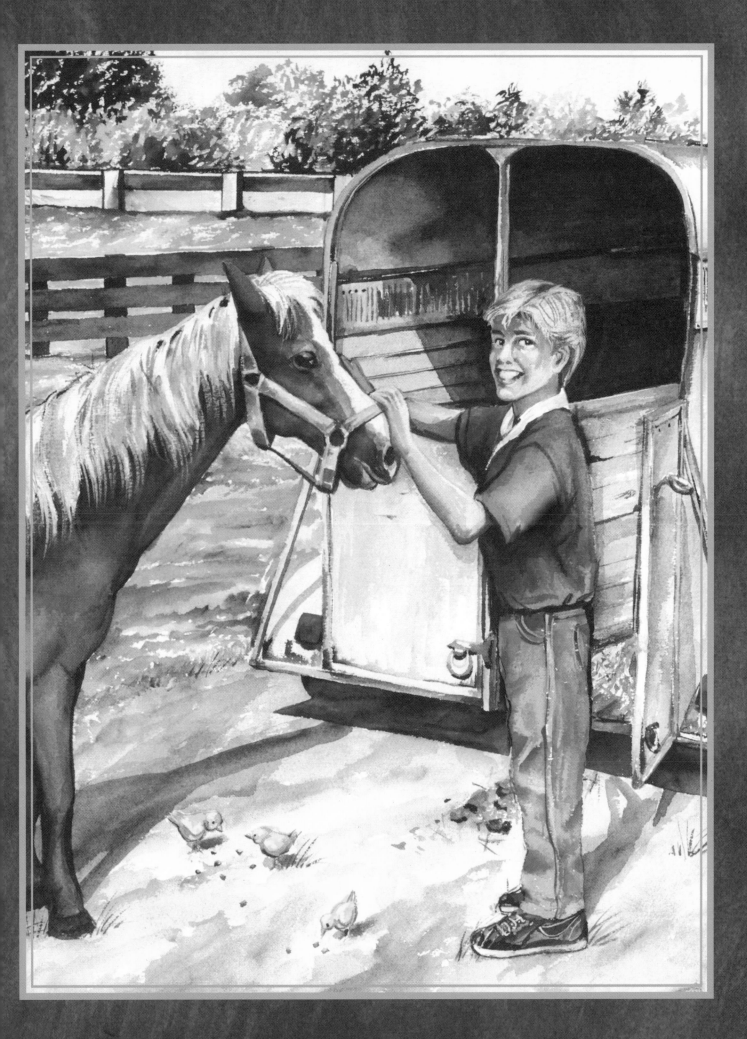

Maria read, *"Do not be deceived: bad company corrupts good morals.* I think it says that if we are always with kids who do bad things, we will end up doing bad things, too."

"You are right, Maria," said Grandpa nodding. "It is important for us to have close friends who know the Lord. This helps to protect us. They will encourage us to do the right things. So remember to choose your friends carefully.

"However, the Lord does not want us to stay away from everyone who does not know Him. In fact, we should be an example to them. You're never too young to be an example. First Timothy 4:12 says it this way: *Don't let anyone look down on you because you are young, but set an example for the believers in speech, in life, in love, in faith and in purity* (NIV). There are people around you all the time who are watching you. This is especially true when it comes to handling money. When you handle money God's way, you are showing others that it can be done."

"But won't being careful about whom we choose as our friends be like playing favorites?" asked Andy with a frown.

"Andy, that is a good question," answered Grandpa. "Carefully choosing close friends because they are good is not the same as playing favorites. Another word for playing favorites is partiality. This is something that the Lord does not want us to do. Andy, why don't you read James 2:1 and 9 for us?"

Andy read, *"Don't show favoritism . . . if you show favoritism, you sin* (NIV). That is pretty clear. It says if we show favoritism we sin."

"That's correct," said Grandpa. "Some people are partial and pay extra attention to those who have a lot of money, are popular or may be good looking. But a person who plays favorites will not treat someone who is poor or unpopular the same way as they treat their friends. The Lord wants us to love all people."

"Grandpa," said Josh. "I know I play favorites sometimes. How can I break this habit?"

Grandpa answered, "Romans 12:10 tells us, *Be devoted to one another in brotherly love; give preference to one another in honor.* And Philippians 2:3 reads, *With humility of mind let each of you regard one another as more important than himself.* These verses mean that we need to ask the Lord to help us to remember to think of each person as more important than ourselves.

"Try to think about the strengths and abilities of each person you know. Everyone can do some things better than we can. Keeping this in mind will help you appreciate all people. It will make you a better example of living God's way."

Just then a green van drove into the driveway. Grandpa said, "Come with me. I want you to meet a very special person."

As they walked toward the van, its side door opened and they could see a girl in a wheelchair. She moved the wheelchair onto a platform and pushed a button that lowered it to the ground.

Grandpa said, "This is Sarah and her mother, Mrs. Martin."

"Hi," said Mrs. Martin.

After greeting Mrs. Martin, the kids turned to Sarah. As Sarah met each of them, her blue eyes lit up and she smiled warmly.

"Why don't you take Sarah out to the barn and show her the clubhouse and animals?" said Grandpa.

"Josh and I can push the wheelchair," volunteered Andy.

As they moved across the yard, Samson came running to meet Sarah. She laughed as he ran around her chair. By the time they reached the barn they were all laughing and talking like old friends.

They showed Sarah the clubhouse. Then they headed towards the field to meet the animals. Soon Grandpa and Mrs. Martin could barely tell the squeals of joy the children were making from the squeals of Abigail's piglets.

When they returned to the porch, Grandpa said, "Well, Sarah, did you enjoy seeing all the animals?"

"They are wonderful," said Sarah. "Maria and Ruth showed me

Shooting Star. He stayed by me the whole time we were in the field. He even nudged the back of my chair. I think he wanted to help Josh and Andy push me."

She turned to her mother and asked, "Can I come to see Shooting Star again, Mom? Please?"

"Yes, Mrs. Martin," Maria joined in. "Can Sarah come again? She can help us do chores. She can be with us in the clubhouse while Grandpa Pete teaches us about money."

"About money?" exclaimed Mrs. Martin. "I would like to learn more about money. Maybe Sarah could learn some things that would help me."

"God wants us all to know how to handle money," said Grandpa. "Why don't you let Sarah stay awhile longer today. She can help the kids finish their chores."

Soon they finished the chores and returned to the porch.

"Mrs. Martin, will Sarah ever be able to walk?" Maria asked quietly.

"We hope so," said Mrs. Martin. "Sarah was born with a hip joint that became too weak to support her weight. Her doctor told us that she could have surgery to replace her hip. Then she would be able to walk again."

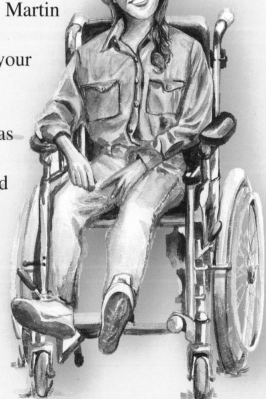

"When will she have the surgery?" asked Ruth.

"As soon as we can afford it, Ruth," Mrs. Martin replied.

"Sarah, it seems like you really enjoyed your visit here today," said Grandpa.

"Oh, I did," said Sarah.

"Sarah, you fit right in with us. It seems as if you have always been here," said Maria.

"Yes," said Andy. "Even the animals liked you. You helped us a lot by measuring the feed for the animals into the pails while we cleaned the pens. We finished the chores a lot faster."

Grandpa smiled. Then he said, "It's kind of like God brought her into our lives, isn't it, kids?"

They looked at Grandpa and then at each other. They all nodded as Josh said, "Sarah, you're God's answer to our prayer. We didn't realize it until now."

"What prayer?" asked Sarah. "What do you mean?"

Grandpa quickly spoke up. "Sarah, we've been praying for a new friend. And God sent you as an answer to that prayer.

"Speaking of answers to prayer," Grandpa continued. "Baseball camp starts in two days. Tomorrow afternoon bring the jars of money you've saved. I will pay you for the work you've done this week. We'll see if you have enough money for camp."

"I can't wait to find out if we can go," said Josh.

"Me, either." replied Grandpa. "And kids, I sense that before you get on the bus to go to camp, you'll discover God's secret for handling money."

Memorize this scripture!

Let no one look down on your youthfulness, but rather in speech, conduct, love, faith and purity, show yourself an example of those who believe (1 Timothy 4:12).

Answer these questions!

1. According to *1 Corinthians 15:33*, do our friends influence us? Why do you think it is important to have godly friends?

_____

_____

2. How can your friends help you handle money wisely?

_____

_____

3. Read *1 Timothy 4:12*. What does this verse say about how you should be an example? _____

_____

4. What are some of the ways you can be an example in handling money in a way that pleases the Lord?_____

_____

5. Look up the word *partiality* in the dictionary. Write down what you think it means. _____

_____

6. Read *Leviticus 19:15* and *James 2:1-9*. What do these passages say about partiality (having favorites)?
Leviticus 19:15 _____

_____

*James 2:1-9*_____

_____

7. Do you choose friends because they have a lot of money, are popular or are good looking? _____

_____

8. Look up *Romans 12:16* and *Philippians 2:3*. How do you think these verses will help you overcome partiality?_____

_____

Work it out!

Think of some ways you can become a wise spender. Read these spending tips:

• Don't carry any more money with you than you need. If you don't have money in your pocket, you won't spend it.

• Do not join music, CD or video clubs. They will end up costing you a lot of money.

• When eating out, drink water for your beverage and have dessert at home.

• Designer clothing is very expensive—avoid buying it!

• All pets cost money. Limit pets to those you really enjoy and can afford.

• Never buy anything through a sales call over the telephone. Many phone sales are dishonest.

• Give and save first, before you spend. Put your savings away as soon as you get your money . . . that way you'll always save more.

Now write down some ways you will spend more wisely:

1. _____
   _____

2. _____
   _____

3. _____
   _____

4. _____
   _____

Get ready for the next chapter! Memorize *Philippians 4:11-12* and answer the questions on pages 93 to 95.

Pray for me! Share your prayer requests with one another and write them down on the Prayer Lists. Then end the lesson by praying.

CHAPTER 11

How Much Is in the Jars?

he kids were excited and a little nervous as they gathered in the clubhouse. "I didn't sleep much last night," Josh told the others. "I hope we have enough money to go to camp. We just have to go."

Just then Grandpa walked into the barn. "Good morning, kids. Why don't we look at our next lesson? After that I'll pay you what I owe you. Then you can count the money in the jars to see if you have enough for camp."

They took out their Bibles while Grandpa continued, "Ruth, do you know what contentment means?"

"I think it means being satisfied or happy with what you have," said Ruth.

"That's very good, Ruth," said Grandpa, nodding. "The Lord wants us to be content with what we have no matter what happens to us.

"Today you're going to find out if you have enough money to go to camp. But what if you don't? Do you think you could be content if you can't go?"

"That would be impossible for me," Josh said, shaking his head.

"I understand how you feel, Josh," Grandpa continued. "But let's look at the apostle Paul. Many difficult things happened to him. Listen to what he said. *[I was] beaten times without number, often in danger of death. Five times I received . . . thirty-nine lashes. Three times I was beaten with rods, once I was stoned, three times I was shipwrecked . . . I have been in labor and hardship, through many sleepless nights, in hunger and thirst, often without food (2 Corinthians 11:23-27)."*

"There is no way he could be content," exclaimed Andy.

"Andy, I think you will be surprised," replied Grandpa. "Read what

Paul said in Philippians 4:11-13. *I have learned to be content in whatever circumstances I am. I know how to get along with humble means, and I also know how to live in prosperity . . . I have learned the secret of being filled and going hungry, both of having abundance and suffering need. I can do all things through Him who strengthens me.*"

"Paul was content no matter what happened to him," Andy said in disbelief. "He was content with a lot of things and with nothing. He was content when things were going well or when bad things happened."

"Maria, do you know where Paul was when he wrote this?" asked Grandpa.

"No," she answered. "Where was he?"

"He was in prison where he was chained to guards day and night," responded Grandpa.

"How can we become content?" asked Josh.

Grandpa smiled and said, "There are several things you should know. First, you need to be faithful. And all of you have been faithful to work hard and save for camp.

"After you have been faithful, you can relax. You can be content because you can be sure the Lord will do the best thing for you. Remember, God loves you. He knows what is best for you. The Lord knows when it will be good for you to have something. He also knows when something might hurt your character."

"Grandpa," Andy began, "does that mean we shouldn't want anything we don't have?"

"No," said Grandpa, smiling. "It just means that we should be content with what we have each day. We can trust God to give us things we don't have when He knows it is the right time.

"Kids, let me ask you a question. What things cause you not to be content?"

"When my friends get new clothes, I am no longer happy

with mine. I want new ones," responded Ruth.

"I am not content when I see some of the commercials on television," said Josh.

"Those are good examples," nodded Grandpa. "Television can be especially dangerous. The average young person spends 30 to 50 hours a week watching TV. They will see about one million commercials by age 20.

"Have you ever taken a close look at the commercials? Everyone seems so happy with what they are trying to sell you. Ads often try to make you discontent. All they really want to do is to get you to spend your money on what they are selling. Think about how much TV you watch. It could harm you more than you realize.

"Now, let's talk about why we should take good care of our bodies. When you ask Jesus to become your Savior, the Spirit of God comes in to live in your body. First Corinthians 3:16 says it this way: *Do you not know that you are a temple of God, and that the Spirit of God dwells in you?*

"It's sad, but many kids start to hurt their bodies because they don't get enough sleep, they eat the wrong food or they don't exercise as they should. Some even drink alcohol or use tobacco or drugs."

"We get enough exercise, don't we?" asked Ruth.

"You sure do," replied Grandpa, laughing. "You play baseball regularly and work hard around here. You should exercise at least three times a week to keep your muscles strong and your body healthy."

"What kinds of food should we eat?" asked Andy.

"What would happen if you put sand in my truck instead of gas?" asked Grandpa. "Do you think it would run well? Of course not. Well, your body works the same way. You need the right fuel to keep it running right.

"You need to eat a balanced diet of protein, vegetables and fruits. Don't eat a steady diet of junk food. Unfortunately, many people eat too much sugar. For example, did you know that there are 12 teaspoons of sugar in one soft drink?

"If most people saved the money they spent on junk food and other unhealthy habits, they would be surprised at the amount of money they could save.

"Talk about savings, take out your jars. Here is the money I owe you for last week's work," said Grandpa, handing money to each kid. "Time to count your money."

They poured out the money and nervously began counting. One by one they found out they had enough. Andy was the last.

"We all have enough for camp!" Andy shouted as soon as he finished counting. "We're going to camp!"

They jumped up and began chanting "We're going to camp! We're going to camp!"

Grandpa clapped his hands. "You deserve to go. You worked so hard and were faithful to give and save," he said grinning.

"God answered our prayers," said Maria. "He is so good."

"Yes, He is good," nodded Grandpa. "Come over early tomorrow and we'll finish our last lesson. Then I'll drive you to the park to meet your teammates at the bus. Sarah is going to be there to say good-bye to you.

"By the way," Grandpa said with a special twinkle in his eyes. "I think you're in for quite a surprise tomorrow."

Memorize this scripture!

For I have learned to be content in whatever circumstances I am. I know how to get along with humble means, and I also know how to live in prosperity (Philippians 4:11-12).

Answer these questions!

1. Look up the word *contentment* in the dictionary. Write down what you think it means. _____

_____

_____

_____

2. What do *Luke 3:14, Philippians 4:11-13, 1 Timothy 6:6-8* and *Hebrews 13:5-6* have to say about contentment?

Luke 3:14 _____

_____

_____

Philippians 4:11-13 _____

_____

_____

1 Timothy 6:6-8 _____

_____

_____

Hebrews 13:5-6 _____

_____

_____

3. Name some things that can make you discontent.

_____

_____

_____

_____

_____

4. Read *1 Corinthians 3:16-17*. If you have asked Jesus Christ into your life, where does God live?_____

_____

_____

_____

5. Since you are a temple that God lives in, how should you take care of your body?_____

_____

_____

_____

6. How do you think that eating nutritious food, exercising and getting enough sleep might save you money in the future?

_____

_____

_____

Work it out!

Learning to be content with what you have will help you become a wise spender. Think about these spending tips.

❏ Enjoy inexpensive hobbies and sports, like time with friends and pick-up basketball games. Try not to confuse shopping with fun.

❏ Pray before you buy anything. Ask the Lord if you really need what you want to buy.

❏ Don't watch too much TV or look at too many magazines. If you do, you'll spend more money.

Make a list of all the junk food you eat this week. Write down some ways you could eat better.

Junk food   What I could eat that would be healthier for me

_____   _____

_____   _____

_____   _____

_____   _____

_____   _____

_____   _____

_____

Get ready for the next chapter! Memorize *Mark 8:36* and answer the questions on pages 102 and 103.

Pray for me! Share your prayer requests with one another and then write them down on the Prayer Lists. Then end the lesson by praying.

CHAPTER 12

The Secret Discovered

Early the next morning the kids met Grandpa on the porch. "I still can't believe we are going to camp!" Josh exclaimed.

"Me, either," said Ruth. "It's like a dream come true."

"I have never seen four more excited kids in my life," said Grandpa, laughing. "Let's go to the clubhouse and finish your last lesson. Then we'll drive over to the bus. Sarah will meet you there to say good-bye."

Once in the clubhouse Grandpa started, "There are two more things you should know about handling money God's way. The first is taxes.

"Andy, do you know what taxes are?"

"Not exactly," Andy said, shaking his head. "But my dad says he has to pay a lot of taxes. And he's not very happy about it."

"I understand," said Grandpa smiling. "Taxes are what we pay the government so that it can do things for us, like build roads. As you get older you will begin paying taxes."

"But do we have to pay taxes?" Andy asked.

"Someone asked Jesus that same question," replied Grandpa. "Turn to Luke 20:24-25 and let's read what He answered. *'Show Me [a Roman coin]. Whose likeness and inscription does it have?' And they said, 'Caesar's.' And He said to them, 'Then render to Caesar the things that are Caesar's.'*

"In other words," Grandpa said, "Jesus said to give to the government what is theirs. Many people try to avoid paying taxes. But that's not what God says. The Bible is clear about our responsibility to pay taxes that are due. *Let every person be in subjection to the governing authorities . . . for rulers are servants of God, devoting themselves to this very thing. Render to all what is due them: tax to*

whom tax is due (Romans 13:1,6-7)."

"Grandpa, I understand about paying taxes," said Josh. "What is the second thing you wanted us to know?"

"We should think about heaven when we spend money," replied Grandpa as he walked to the door of the barn. "Come over here, kids. Do you see the line I drew in the dirt the whole length of the barn?"

"Yes, but what does it mean?" asked Josh.

"This might be hard for you kids to believe," answered Grandpa, "but your life on earth is short. Psalm 90:10 tells us, *The length of our days is seventy years — or eighty* (NIV). When you compare that with how long we will be together with God in heaven, it is very short.

"Right in the middle of this long line I put a penny," said Grandpa, bending down. "The little penny represents our time on earth. The long line represents the millions and millions of years we will be in heaven.

"And here is what is important to understand. How you spend your money during your life on earth will count forever. When you spend money in ways that please the Lord, He will reward you in heaven. You can either spend money helping others, or you can always spend selfishly on yourself.

"Remember what we learned in our first lesson. If we spend money God's way, we will grow closer to Him. Nothing in life is more precious than knowing the Lord better. Mark 8:36 says it this way, *For what does it profit a man to gain the whole world, and forfeit his soul?*"

Just then Grandma called from the porch, "Mrs. Martin needs to talk to you right away. Sarah needs help."

Grandpa ran to the house.

When he returned Josh asked in a worried voice, "How is Sarah?"

"She's not doing well," Grandpa answered. "Last night her hip was in such pain she couldn't sleep. The doctor said she needed to have the hip replaced right away. But they don't have enough money for the surgery."

Maria went over to stand beside him. "Grandpa," she said as a big tear rolled down her cheek. "I want Sarah to be able to walk. I think she was the answer to our prayer that God would give us somebody to help. But we haven't helped her with her biggest need. What can we do?"

"Let's ask God to show us what we can do to help," said Grandpa.

They bowed their heads. Each of them prayed, asking God to show them what they could do. As they finished, Josh said softly, "I know something we can do."

"What is it?" Andy asked.

"Sarah wants to walk more than anything else in the world. But she doesn't have enough money for her operation. We've saved a lot of money so that we could go to baseball camp. I don't know how much her operation costs, but I want to give her the money I saved so she can have her operation."

Immediately Ruth spoke up. "Josh, what a wonderful idea. I wanted to go to camp more than anything else just a few weeks ago. But now I want to see Sarah walk more than I want to go to camp. I want to give my money, too."

"Me, too," said Maria.

Andy came closer to Grandpa. His face was very serious. He stood quietly for a minute. Then he said, "I've never been to baseball camp before. I've been waiting for the time to come for weeks. But since we met Sarah, camp doesn't seem as important. I think God wants me to give my money, too. Camp will just have to wait."

Grandpa sat quietly, looking from one face to another. His voice shook a little as he said, "You've done it! You discovered the secret of God's way of handling money. Remember the verse you memorized from Acts 20:35, *It is more blessed to give than to receive*. You found out it is true. It is more of a blessing for you to give to Sarah than to receive even something you want badly."

Grandpa wiped the tears from his eyes. He said, "Now, I have a surprise. During the past few weeks you have helped me with the work. You have studied hard to learn what God says about money. But today you have shown me that you're willing to sacrifice something you wanted very badly to help someone in need."

He paused a minute, then continued. "Now you are about to receive a blessing." He pulled a piece of paper out of his pocket and handed it to Josh. "Read this, Josh."

A puzzled expression came over Josh's face. "What is this all about?" he asked. "This is your picture. It is an advertisement for Pete Nelson's Little League Baseball Camp. That's you, Grandpa; you are Pete Nelson."

Andy grabbed the paper from Josh's hand. "It is you. What does it mean when it says it is your camp?"

"Well, years ago I decided to start a camp for young baseball players. Several of my friends who are major leaguers agreed to help me. I thought we should make the camp available to the Little League players here in town. It's my camp that you have been saving your money to attend. Since you gave your money to Sarah for her operation, I want you to attend camp as my guests."

They couldn't believe their ears. They stared in amazement at Grandpa. Then they erupted in shouts of happiness as they fell onto the hay and rolled around in joy.

Grandpa laughed so hard his baseball cap fell to the floor. Then he said, "Well, kids, shall we call Sarah?"

They jumped to their feet and dashed toward the house. Andy stopped to say, "Grandpa, it really does make me happy to give Sarah my money."

"Yes, Andy," Grandpa said as he put his arm around Andy's shoulder. "It truly is more blessed to give than to receive."

Later that day they gathered at the park with the rest of the team. Their suitcases were packed and they were ready to go. Grandpa was dressed in his major league baseball jersey. They were just about to board the bus for the trip to camp.

Suddenly, they saw Mrs. Martin's van pulling into the parking lot. Sarah was waving her arm out the window.

"Maria, Ruth, Josh, Andy," she called as they ran to the van.

"I had to come and tell you something," said Sarah. Her blue eyes danced with excitement. "Guess what?" she teased her friends.

"What, Sarah, tell us?" Maria begged.

"By the time you come back from camp I will have a new hip. My doctor says if everything goes all right, I will be able to start to walk in just six weeks. I never could have had the operation if you hadn't helped me. I've never had any friends that meant as much to me as you."

Grandpa stood quietly listening. As Sarah finished, he said, "Six weeks ago I would never have guessed that you would have learned so much about God's ways of handling money. I'm very proud of you. And I am sure God is pleased, too."

Then he glanced toward the bus where all the other campers were waiting to go. "Time to go," he said. "Let's go to camp!"

"Thanks for everything!" Sarah called as they ran to the bus.

Grandpa smiled as he jogged toward the bus. "Yes, God," he said quietly, "Thanks for everything!"

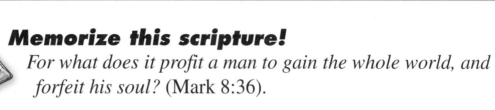

Memorize this scripture!

For what does it profit a man to gain the whole world, and forfeit his soul? (Mark 8:36).

Answer these questions!

1. What are taxes?_____

_____

_____

_____

2. Read *Matthew 22:17-21* and *Romans 13:1-7*. Do you think the Lord wants us to pay the government taxes that we owe them? Why?

_____

_____

_____

3. How would you define *eternity*? _____

_____

_____

_____

4. Moses was rich when he was growing up. Read *Hebrews 11:24-26*. Why do you think Moses chose to suffer rather than to remain rich?

_____

_____

_____

_____

_____

5. Do you think Moses will be happy in heaven because he made this decision? Why?_____

_____

_____

_____

_____

6. Look up *Mark 8:36*. What do you think this verse means?

_____

_____

_____

7. Describe the most helpful part of this entire study to you.

_____

_____

_____

_____

Work it out!

Advertisers spend millions of dollars trying to get you to buy things. It is important to learn some of their tricks they use to get you to spend money.

Think about this. In most ads the people are smiling and seem so happy. In magazines they use pretty pictures. On TV they use music in the ads to get you to buy what they are selling.

Now look at some ads. Write down how the ads try to get you to spend money.

What are they selling?	What tricks are they using in the ad?
_____	_____
_____	_____
_____	_____
_____	_____
_____	_____

Pray for me! Take prayer requests from one another and write them down on the Prayer Lists. Then end the lesson by praying.

PRAYER LIST

Name: _____   Parents: _____

Home Phone: _____   Brothers And Sisters: _____

Home Address: _____   _____

_____   _____

_____   _____

Chapter	Prayer Requests	Answers To Prayers
1		
2		
3		
4		
5		
6		
7		
8		
9		
10		
11		
12		

"Pray for one another" James 5:16

PRAYER LIST

Name: _____ Parents: _____

Home Phone: _____ Brothers And Sisters: _____

Home Address: _____ _____

_____ _____

_____ _____

Chapter	Prayer Requests	Answers To Prayers
1		
2		
3		
4		
5		
6		
7		
8		
9		
10		
11		
12		

"Pray for one another" James 5:16

PRAYER LIST

Name: _____ Parents: _____

Home Phone: _____ Brothers And Sisters: _____

Home Address: _____ _____

_____ _____

_____ _____

Chapter	Prayer Requests	Answers To Prayers
1		
2		
3		
4		
5		
6		
7		
8		
9		
10		
11		
12		

"Pray for one another" James 5:16

PRAYER LIST

Name: _____ Parents: _____

Home Phone: _____ Brothers And Sisters: _____

Home Address: _____ _____

_____ _____

_____ _____

Chapter	Prayer Requests	Answers To Prayers
1		
2		
3		
4		
5		
6		
7		
8		
9		
10		
11		
12		

"Pray for one another" James 5:16

PRAYER LIST

Name: _____   Parents: _____

Home Phone: _____   Brothers And Sisters: _____

Home Address: _____   _____

_____   _____

_____   _____

Chapter	Prayer Requests	Answers To Prayers
1		
2		
3		
4		
5		
6		
7		
8		
9		
10		
11		
12		

"Pray for one another" James 5:16

PRAYER LIST

Name: _____   Parents: _____

Home Phone: _____   Brothers And Sisters: _____

Home Address: _____   _____

_____   _____

_____   _____

Chapter	Prayer Requests	Answers To Prayers
1		
2		
3		
4		
5		
6		
7		
8		
9		
10		
11		
12		

"Pray for one another" James 5:16

PRAYER LIST

Name: _____   Parents: _____

Home Phone: _____   Brothers And Sisters: _____

Home Address: _____   _____

_____   _____

_____   _____

Chapter	Prayer Requests	Answers To Prayers
1		
2		
3		
4		
5		
6		
7		
8		
9		
10		
11		
12		

"Pray for one another" James 5:16

Since 1894, Moody Publishers has been dedicated to equip and motivate people to advance the cause of Christ by publishing evangelical Christian literature and other media for all ages, around the world. Because we are a ministry of the Moody Bible Institute of Chicago, a portion of the proceeds from the sale of this book go to train the next generation of Christian leaders.

If we may serve you in any way in your spiritual journey toward understanding Christ and the Christian life, please contact us at www.moodypublishers.com.

"All Scripture is God-breathed and is useful for teaching, rebuking, correcting and training in righteousness, so that the man of God may be thoroughly equipped for every good work."

—2 TIMOTHY 3:16, 17

CROWN FINANCIAL MINISTRIES

Teaching People God's Financial Principles

In September 2000, Christian Financial Concepts and Crown Minstries of Orlando, Florida were brought together in the ministry marriage now known as Crown Financial Ministries.

The union of these two ministries created an alliance that is having far-reaching impact on the church in America and around the world. The purpose of the ministry is to teach people God's financial principles in order to know Christ more intimately and to be free to serve Him.